CAT
CONDOMINIUMS
AND OTHER
FELINE FURNITURE

By the same authors

CAT CONDOMINIUMS

AND OTHER
FELINE FURNITURE

George Ney with
Susan Sherman Fadem

FOREWORD BY ELLEN SAWYER

 E. P. DUTTON   NEW YORK

To Ed Zerr,
who helped keep the Cat House business going

Published in the United States by E. P. Dutton,
a division of Penguin Books USA Inc.,
2 Park Avenue, New York, N.Y. 10016

Published simultaneously in Canada by
Fitzhenry and Whiteside, Limited, Toronto.

Library of Congress Cataloging-in-Publication Data

Ney, George.
Cat condominiums and other feline furniture / George Ney with
Susan Sherman Fadem. — 1st ed.
p.   cm.
ISBN 0-525-48430-2
1. Cats—Equipment and supplies.   2. Cats—Housing.   I. Fadem,
Susan Sherman.   II. Title.
SF447.3.N49   1989
636.8'083—dc19   88-14965
                                                            CIP

Designed by Earl Tidwell

Photographs by Mark Hodges, unless otherwise specified
Construction plans by Gunners Mate 1st Class Richard J. Smith,
United States Navy

10 9 8 7 6 5 4 3 2

Contents

Illustrations

CONSTRUCTION PLANS

Foreword

Our cats are wild about George Ney's cat houses. We wouldn't use any other kind. Rather than a people's version of what cats might want, the houses are built from a cat's viewpoint.

Our cats gravitate to the houses immediately; they love the curves, the comfort, and the natural feeling of the tree limbs. We have about 175 cats at a time, and 19 George Ney cat houses.

—ELLEN SAWYER
Executive Director
Tree House Animal Foundation
Chicago, Illinois*

*The Tree House Animal Foundation operates a cage-free adoption and treatment center for homeless animals.

1
The Cat's Own Place

A couple in Wisconsin had a house full of cats. The cats in turn had a house of their own. A George Ney Kitty Duplex, it was a large carpeted box partitioned down the middle and mounted on a tree limb.

In the duplex, for hours on end, the cats would snooze and play.

The cats were quite happy, the couple knew. The husband and wife were not nearly so happy, the cats may well have known.

One day the couple divorced. Included in the property settlement were the cats, the family's home, and the Kitty Duplex. The ex-wife, who took most of the cats, agreed to leave the family's home. The ex-husband got the rest of the cats, and also the couple's home. And for his felines' continued happiness and security, the ex-husband got the Kitty Duplex.

Tough Cat, a Chicagoan, is likewise attached to his George Ney Deluxe Tunnel of Love cat house—a carpeted tunnel, two carpeted perches, and a three-foot-high tree-limb scratching post. However, T.C. (as the Himalayan seal point is known for short) is too plump for long jumps. He weighs twenty-two pounds.

To reach his beloved perch, T.C. has devised an ingenious system. First, he heaves himself onto a chair. From the chair, he lumbers onto a desk. Then, like a bloated trapeze artist in search of a trapeze, he lurches upward until his front claws plop down on the edge of the carpeted perch. His hind legs, meanwhile, are dangling. To hoist them, T.C. summons super-cat strength. Digging his toenails/front claws into the perch, he bears down mightily and pulls up his hulking frame. Like a triple serving of Jell-O, T.C. spills over the carpeted perch. Exhausted, he dozes. He awakens, squirms, and falls back to sleep—all on the perch.

What T.C. and all cats know instinctively, the Wisconsin divorcé understood, and you are about to discover, is that cats need a place of their own. They need a dependable dozing pad, a spot that won't be buried under books, newspapers, or the dirty laundry the next time the cat craves a catnap.

Likewise, cats need a place, other than a chair leg or couch bottom, where they can scratch without restriction and without an "Oh, my God, look what he's done now!" wail from humans.

Moreover, felines need a secure retreat. This is don't-touch-me territory where pets can hotfoot it away from gushy, cat-loving dinner guests, curious toddlers, and the world at large.

All this and a cat's inherent fondness for nature-watching and heights were driven home to me quite by accident about a dozen years ago. That's when—again, quite by accident—I made the prototypes of what was to become the country's most extensive line of cat furniture. To date, my company has sold more than ten thousand cat houses—as I call them—in designs ranging from the Deluxe Scratch Pad to the Tunnel of Love, the Royal Cat-sle, and the Southern Plantation House for Aristo-cats.

All materials in every cat house are chosen to please cats first, and then humans. One finicky two-legged female from Illinois was worried that no feline of hers could be happy with a cat house. A dry run was mandatory, she concluded. Contacting her understanding neighborhood pet shop owner, who had in stock about a dozen of my cat houses, the woman requested that the pet shop be closed briefly to the public. During this quiet interlude, the woman said, she would bring her cat to the shop and observe its reaction to the cat houses. Amused, the tolerant pet shop owner consented.

The woman and the cat arrived. Instantly the cat jumped into a little carpeted house on a Double-Perch Kitty Tree House. Ten minutes later, the tree house was carried to the woman's car. So was the cat; it was still inside the little house.

The *Chicago Tribune* has hailed my cat houses as "the Ritz of cat posts." *USA Today* called my designer cat condos "the cat's meow."

Every George Ney cat house has tree limbs incorporated into it. A tree is a cat's natural scratching post. In the wilds, long before there were blueprints for do-it-yourself cat houses, felines of all sizes and savagery were scratching against trees. The scent of the wood attracted them; it still does.

So does the outdoors. Ordinarily, scrunched onto windowsills and craning over ferns, cats gaze out the window. But unhassled, on a perch all his own, a feline with a cat house has a comfy, reserved seat for nature's twenty-four-hour television show. From a cat house, pulled close to a

The author with a tall tree house. "Every George Ney cat house incorporates tree limbs."

window, cats can safely watch and periodically salivate over an endless parade of squawking birds, bugs, ravenous squirrels, field mice, snakes, and ducks.

Cats are also crazy about heights. When was the last time you saw your cat on the floor? More likely, and given its druthers, the cat was on a stool, the dining-room table, a kitchen counter, or the mantel. Again, cat houses accommodate such passions.

One midwestern feline was particularly frustrated. He was devoted to a successful businesswoman with a majestic home. The living room had spectacular, lofty cathedral ceilings, beneath which enticing square rafters bridged the room. The cat would often sit on the back of a chair, eyeing the rafters wistfully. He would gather himself for a spring, but then sit back in frustration, knowing he could not reach the inviting rafter.

Aware that her pet had been pouting, the businesswoman came to me with a $100 roll of pale green carpeting. "Please, build something to make my cat happy," she pleaded.

Warming to my mission, I located a noteworthy seven-foot-long tree limb. To the limb I anchored a pale green carpeted tunnel, a little sloping-roofed house, and five customized perches. Usually my cat house perches are eighteen inches long. But knowing this was a forlorn bachelor cat— living without feline companionship as he tried to claw his way to the rafters—I lopped some inches off a couple of perches. Instead of eighteen-inch lounges, they became six- and twelve-inch stepping-stones.

My bill to the woman was $200. (If you as a do-it-yourselfer tackle a less lofty project, your costs would be far less.) My bill naturally did not include what the woman had paid for the pale green carpeting. But both she and the cat were tickled pink with their new acquisition.

The units you are about to build can range from a foot or two high to five feet or so from the floor. From bottom to top, in stepladder fashion, the units have a cat-pleasing

Kerri Smith, aged eight, shares a Ney racing car with my cat Scupa.

assortment of tunnels, roofs with skylight/air conditioners, and perches. Often, by leaping, hopping, and otherwise hoisting themselves onto and into such components, felines all but lose their yearnings for your piano, your bookcase . . .

And except when the humans involved happen to prefer plywood, all my cat house perches, tunnels, and tubes are made of sturdy paperboard tubing. Think of feline physiques. Whether a svelte Siamese, or a he-man like T.C., cats seem to feel secure with something that curves around them.

Katz Koop Pete, a silvery American shorthair, is blind. More than six years ago, he lost his sight. Although he lives with other cats at Katz Koop cattery in Northlake, Illinois, Pete doesn't socialize much. Mostly he stays in the sturdy tube of his Skylight over Kitty Land cat house.

"Pete seems quite content having something over him. The other cats know the tube belongs to him. Nobody else bothers it," says Hazel Gellinger, Pete's human.

Pete's tube is carpeted. So are all surfaces—with the exception of tree limbs and bottoms of plywood bases—in my cat houses. Cats cling to carpeting. They squirm on it, scratch on it, and rub their sides, bellies, and backs on it.

Mia Lee and Schroeder Lee, a mother and son Siamese cat duo, sleep side by side on a carpeted Deluxe Scratch Pad. They doze on their backs, paws pointing upward, tails hanging down. Mia Lee and Schroeder Lee live with the Hochstadter family in Oak Park, Illinois.

Until now, my cat houses have been available primarily at cat shows from coast to coast and in Canada, and at pet shops within the Chicago area. Prices range from $25 for a Deluxe Scratch Pad, to $175 for a Perch for Feline Swingers and $225 for a Kitty Duplex. Customized models run somewhat higher.

For many people, seeing the obvious pleasure their cats derive from the cat houses, price is no deterrent. A couple in Germantown, Wisconsin, has ordered at least one cat house for each room of their new home. The couple has twelve Silver Tabbies.

A man in Chicago has three cats. He owns seven of my cat houses.

A cat-loving midwestern therapist, finding that cats had a calming influence on her not always calm clients, redecorated her office. She bought four cat houses for the four corners of her consulting room and moved in her cats.

Frequently I am asked how I build such cat houses. Because I've never seen any reason to be secretive, I always reply, giving a brief rundown of supplies and construction techniques.

But behind these inquiries, and motivating me to write this book, are the often unasked questions: Well, couldn't I build these cat houses myself, and at a fraction of the cost?

To be perfectly honest, since you don't have the overhead of running a business, and the need to make a living, there's no reason why you can't construct an appealing, even downright irresistible cat house. And if you are a resourceful scavenger, scrounger, or buyer of reasonably priced materials, your costs should not exceed a couple of dollars for a scratching post, or any more than $50 or so for the most elaborate of cat houses.

And as a do-it-yourselfer plus a cat lover, you will reap additional benefits. Just imagine your cat sprawled out in his very own Catnip Saloon cat house, snoozing and/or basking in the sunlight.

Happiness. Peace. And won't your feline be over-whelmed with gratitude?

Fat chance. Cats firmly believe that they don't have to thank us for anything. Long ago they concluded that what-ever we do for them, we should have done it earlier. When-ever we give them something, even if it's today, it's always a day too late. And whatever we give them, it's nothing more or less than they deserve.

With cat houses, however, cats are right. More than a dozen years in the business have shown me that every feline deserves one or more lovingly executed, handmade, purr-sonal cat houses. Among satisfied recipients:

Two jet-setter cats were in the habit of traveling to Flor-ida with their owners, both licensed pilots. Although the couple's plane could easily have accommodated cat carriers, the free-spirited felines wanted no part of such confinement. Instead, the cats blissfully passed each flight scampering from cabin to cockpit and cockpit to cabin. Fatigued, the cats would then doze upon available laps and arms. Unfor-tunately, these belonged to the pilot and copilot.

Distraught, the couple came to me. Concerned with the safety of all aboard, they requested ersatz feline airline seats. Even though my personal means of transportation has long been a van, I obliged. Guided by the dimensions of the airplane, I took several small tree limbs and between them securely nailed two carpeted perches and a small carpeted tunnel. For the Deluxe Tunnel of Love, the price was $60.

The couple wedged the cat house into the back of the plane. They hoped the cats would be so enthralled by the Tunnel of Love that they would mostly stay away from the navigational controls.

The strategy worked. The last I heard, the cats were still romping and sleeping on their airborne perches, and the pilots were still piloting distraction-free.

Then there's Tender Vittles. She has arthritis. Tender Vittles is a favorite feline at Lambs Farm, a small residential facility and shopping area operated for mentally handicapped adults in Libertyville, Illinois.

Before Tender Vittles's joints began to ache, the house parent at Lambs Farm bought her a Tunnel of Love cat house with a perch two feet from the floor. To the continuing fascination of residents, Tender Vittles would spend at least part of each day scratching on the tree limb, jumping up on the perch, and sleeping.

When arthritis set in, Tender Vittles could still leap up. But every time she jumped down from her perch, the veterinarian confirmed, the cat experienced pain.

The house parent and the other residents could not imagine Tender Vittles facing life without her cat house. Instead, they ordered a down-size model. A miniature version of the original, it measures just over twelve inches high.

Once again Tender Vittles jumps up and down with ease.

Your cat will, too.

2
Ney and the Cat House Business

Tell someone you're in the cat house business, and it's bound to raise eyebrows. But truthfully, my entrepreneurial intentions are strictly honorable.

Somehow I was backed into this line of work, prodded by a tree limb, roundabout compliments, and an occasionally wacky sense of how to make a living. Earlier, I had turned myself into a human tractor. To level the ground for a nine-hole golf course, I once spent hours dragging around a piece of lumber.

At other times I've operated a pint-size summer resort, sold furniture, run a twenty-four-hour truck-stop restaurant, and sold tile and carpeting. Through each of these ventures, I never lost hope that one day I would actually make money.

For a while I was certain the gold mine would be my tile and carpet store in Fox River Grove, a wisp of a town in northern Illinois. As new construction boomed, so did my sales. Supremely confident, I opened two more stores.

But then calamity struck in the form of the oil shortage of the 1970s. Interest rates skyrocketed. With contractors idled, the building business was literally in shambles.

Needless to say, virtually no one was buying my tiles and carpeting. Besides a large inventory at the store, I was left with an increasingly unbalanced ledger. Normally unflappable, I panicked.

To preserve my sanity during the mostly customer-free days, I invented a project. I took empty oversize spools discarded by electrical companies and covered them with unsold plush carpeting. To me, the results were recreation-room furniture—tailor-made for anyone needing carpeted end tables, carpeted lamp tables, or carpeted cocktail tables.

Passersby thought otherwise. "Gee, that would make a good scratching post for my cat," a number of people said. Dumbfounded, but too strapped financially to be insulted, I agreed.

Feline-related comments continued. Finally, after being hit over the head often enough with the same idea, I got one of my own: I would build an entire line of cat furniture.

As jubilant as anyone can be who is on the verge of bankruptcy, I became a regular customer of the lumberyard across the street. I would buy strips of plywood and plywood bases, carpet them from my never-ending inventory, and securely nail the pieces together. The final product I called a cat scratching post.

Sales didn't quite go through the roof. But at least I kept busy.

One day a woman walked in. I'll never forget her. For her cat, she wanted an especially nice piece of furniture. Hungry to please, I fashioned a three-tier plywood scratching post.

It was summer. When I made the delivery, alongside her

house was a tree limb with branches shooting out in every direction. That's when it hit me. Suddenly I could envision turning that limb into something phenomenal for cats. Here in front of my eyes was a one-of-a-kind scratching post. The whole way home I could barely keep my eyes on the road. In every sturdy limb, in every fascinating branch, I saw a scratching post. I still do.

On and off since I was a kid in St. Louis, Michigan, I'd had a cat, although I didn't have one at that moment. Besides affection and food, I'd always given cats the run of my life. In other words, my cats ruled me. But as much as I cared about cats, I'd never thought of accumulating many actual possessions for them. At that point I'd never made or bought a cat of mine a special perch or scratching post.

However, I realized that all cats scratch, or at least go through the motions. For cats, scratching serves a definite purpose. It helps whittle down a feline's claws, which continue to grow, just like a human's fingernails. Even if cats have been declawed, they still scratch, primarily to relieve the occasional itching on the pads on their paws. These pads, which all cats have, are like calluses on a human hand. Sometimes they need scratching.

Indoors, to the periodic chagrin of owners, many felines use the furniture for these purposes. Outdoors, cats scratch on trees.

Embellishing on nature, to each retrieved tree limb I began to add a carpeted plywood perch—sometimes, several perches. Cats, I knew, loved heights. Therefore, I reasoned that it might be just as pleasurable for cats—and pleasing to owners, too—if the cats could leap onto their own personal carpeted perches, instead of onto the kitchen table or into the baby's high chair.

For a change, my thinking was on target. As cat furniture buyers reported, not only were their pets jumping onto my carpeted perches, but they were scratching on them, playing on them, yawning, curling up in a ball on them, stretching out, and snoozing.

Cats were stretching out and snoozing on my perches.

What's more, the longer the cats spent on the cat furniture, the less time they spent using—and sometimes abusing—other furniture in the home or apartment.

Soon my creations went from practical to practical-but-posh, then even more posh. From knee-high scratching post/perches, I began building multitier tree houses with contoured perches two feet, four feet, and even five feet from the ground.

Once I took a special order from a rare-coin dealer whose spacious, high-ceilinged log cabin overlooked a lake in Wisconsin. His cats were crazy about playing on the second-floor balcony, he told me. To speed their ascent and descent, he wanted two seven-foot-high scratching posts. At regular intervals on each post, I hammered a perch, a total of four perches per post. That way the cats could bypass the log cabin's staircase, bound from perch to perch, and sprint onto the balcony, all—should the cats desire—within seconds. Only the delivery took time. It took three of us to load and unload those scratching posts into my van.

But I wasn't complaining. In what was to be the very first of well over 750 newspaper stories that mentioned the cat furniture, the *Herald* in suburban Chicago proclaimed: "Ney's work is sure to win a Cheshire grin." Photos of my feline "architectural environments" and "cat accouterments" covered nearly half a page in the paper.

Later, the *News-Examiner* in Gallatin, Tennessee, would call my kitty cottages "designer cat houses." The *Post-Bulletin* in Rochester, Minnesota, said I was trying to build up "a kitty" and put it into cat houses.

For years people had given their cats fluffy or velvety pillows ensconced in cardboard cartons or kitty-size brass and wicker beds. Moreover, many carpeted plywood scratching posts were already on the market. But as one reporter put it, I may well have been the first to wed tree limbs to feline dozing, scratching, and nature watching, and then to try to sell my memorable creations.

Just how memorable, I was dying to know. Encouraged in particular by one satisfied two-legged client, I decided to test my wares at a cat show in Appleton, Wisconsin. All I had to lose, I figured, was the show's twenty-five-dollar booth rental fee, plus gasoline for my battered van.

The Appleton show hall was teeming with immaculately groomed purebred felines. They gloated. They purred, and they won ribbon after ribbon. But I was a show-stopper, too. Even the most indulgent of cat owners had never seen anything like my furniture. I sold one Kitty Duplex (the one that later went to the ex-husband in the divorce settlement) and four scratching posts.

Shortly afterward, I went to the North Shore Cat Club show in Grayslake, Illinois. Again the crowd was flabbergasted. This time I sold out. One woman alone special-ordered four pieces of furniture.

Thrilled, I rented space at the Jolly Roger Cat Show in Chicago. Customers swarmed around, but not nearly enough to wipe out my outstanding debts. I was bankrupt. And summoning every ounce of guts and blind faith, I finally acknowledged that even if my tile and carpet business could be revived, I wasn't the one to do it. I was no longer interested.

I've always said that when God was making all the animals, he saved cats for last so he could get all the bugs out first. Now I decided to hitch my future to the tail of a cat. Although friends said I was crazy, I've never looked back. In January 1980, I did what seemed to me the only sane thing to do. Mesmerized by the idea of creating something cats would enjoy, I opened near my home in Mundelein, Illinois, what may well have been the first shop in the country to deal exclusively in cat furniture.

"Me-e-e-ow-w-w-w," I answered the phone at the shop, and still do. I named the shop Cat House Originals.

The name never fails to get a reaction. If it gets a sale, I'm even happier.

3
Branching
Out

My shop was no Saks Fifth Avenue. I subleased a small part of an already small building from a specialty advertising company. Into it I dumped tree limbs, plywood, and carpet. I also brought in tools—some of the last visible reminders of my years in the tile and carpet business.

All day I would blast away with my power saw, pneumatic stapler, and hammer. On weekends, I would pile a week's output of cat furniture into my battered van and start driving. These travels were to become part of an annual 40,000-mile journey to and from cat shows across the United States and into Canada.

In those days, I was the chief driver, van-packer, and entire sales force for Cat House Originals. I was also chief architect and upholsterer. My only helper was Jack Brady. In

At work in the Cat House Originals shop (Courtesy Southwest News-Sun, *Libertyville, Illinois; Lem Case Photo)*

his seventies, Jack was retired. I'd bring wood and trees into his garage. He'd build the units, and I'd upholster them back at my shop. Up until the time Jack died of a heart attack, he was still building cat houses.

My sales pattern was to stick mostly with cat shows sponsored by such organizations as the Cat Fanciers' Association and American Cat Fanciers' Association. From Birmingham to Milwaukee, Kansas City, and Omaha, I booked booth space in community centers, hotels, schools, and convention halls.

A cat show, I quickly learned, is the feline equivalent of the Hollywood Oscars. Amid howling, hoopla, and the popping of flashbulbs, such remarkably named specimens as Lupracan Mus Flower Drum Song and Etcetera's Bullwrinkle compete for grand championships, satiny ribbons, and kudos. Immaculately groomed and resplendent, the felines themselves ranged from inherently scrawny to meticulously fluffed and puffed.

The number of spectators per weekend varied, too, from hundreds to thousands. The bigger shows at Madison Square Garden in New York, the Cow Palace in San Francisco, and Place Bonaventure in Montreal, Canada, attracted up to twenty thousand people. To me, every showgoer—whether two- or four-legged—was a potential cat house sale.

Unfortunately, there was lots of competition for the onlooker's dollar. Temptations included catnip-stuffed toy mice, kitty cookies, and pastel velour slipcovers for litter boxes. To all this, I added natural tree limbs and carpeted perches. Although copycats have since entered the field, when I went into business, there was nothing like my cat houses on the market.

From my small booth at cat shows, boughs cum scratching posts would jut in every direction, making my display almost impossible to miss. This was to my advantage.

If show halls were jam-packed enough, some cat lovers would literally bump into my wares. Others required a not-so-subtle prod. "Young lady, your cat needs a cat house," I would boldly announce to a woman of any age, and preferably to one who was clear across the room.

I wanted heads to turn. The more people heard about the cat houses, the greater the chance they would check out my booth. In order to offer cats something they could sink their claws into, I was making a career "out of craziness," as the *Philadelphia Inquirer* later put it.

Meanwhile, certain questions became routine: What if I buy a cat house and my cat doesn't like it? Skepticism from first-time buyers was pardonable. Still, I believed so implicitly in my product that I made—and continue to make—an offer even General Motors cannot beat: Buy the cat house. And if your cat is not perfectly satisfied, return the house the next time I'm in town. I'll give you a full refund.

To my knowledge, only three houses have ever been returned. All three I donated to animal shelters where, so far as I know, they are still in use.

As the cat houses and I became known commodities on the cat-show circuit, one of my biggest thrills was returning weeks or months later to a city for another cat show and finding onetime skeptics lined up to buy their second and third cat houses.

Some weekends, strictly from sales of $35 and $85 carpeted perches, I went home with $400 to $500 in my pocket. Once in Wichita, Kansas, I sold nearly $700 worth of cat furniture. For a guy fighting his way back in the business world, this was an absolute fortune. Driving home in my empty van, I was on top of the world.

Still, there were times when I didn't have two nickels to rub together. One week, disappointing sales left me with no money to buy plywood for perches.

However, in what turned out to be an act of fortuitous desperation, I raided my own leftovers. Still in my shop, left over from a couple of kitty hot rods and cat-size World War I biplanes, were the remains of several thick paperboard tubes. The tubes of course were round. On the sudden hunch that a rounded paperboard perch might be even more comfortable for cats than a flat plywood one, I carpeted the tubes and attached them to tree-limb scratching posts.

At the next cat show, the furniture with contoured perches practically flew out of the booth.

Demand finally increased to the point that I needed help. A classified ad in one of the Chicago area papers caught my eye. Ed Zerr, retired after forty-two years as a food broker, was looking for odd jobs. Working for Cat House Originals, I figured, would more than fit the bill.

Ed is a dapper, cultured gentleman. His tastes run to bow ties and tweeds. I'm more on the rustic side. (In one of my favorite descriptions, the *Herald-Telephone* newspaper in Bloomington, Indiana, later said of me: "Clad in denim overalls, a jean jacket and cowboy boots—and peering through a pair of black-rimmed glasses shaded by the broad brim of a cowboy hat—Ney looks as if he just fell off a potato truck.")

Yet despite our differences, Ed and I hit it off immediately. And when he said my cat houses were "sort of artistic," how could I help but hire him?

Ours has proved to be a lasting association. Ed has not only built and designed thousands of cat houses but has gone in the van with the cat houses and me to countless cat shows. One show he remembers in particular.

A friend in the tree business had saved us a humongous tree trunk. It must have been six feet tall, with five or six limbs still attached. From limb tip to limb tip, the whole thing probably measured eight feet wide. For weeks the tree trunk gathered dust until one day Ed added carpeted perches, tunnels, and houses.

The effect was unforgettable—so much so that at a cat show one woman kept returning to our booth. The woman had four cats; she couldn't take her eyes off the tree-trunk colossus, which we had priced at $150. Whenever spectators surged toward the booth, the woman would join them, then retreat.

After considerable pondering, she bought the piece. Somehow Ed and I managed to tie part of it into her car trunk, branches radiating out behind like a miniforest gone through a buzz saw. Days later, Ed and I received a thank-you note; the woman's cats loved the tree house.

Elsewhere, relationships were far icier. When the ad agency in my building requested more space, I was the one who moved—this time to downtown Mundelein. The new quarters were disastrous. I shared space with a locksmith. He occupied one side of the store; I got the other. We shared a common entrance. We also shared a window, or so I thought. When I displayed my cat houses in "our" window, he seemed perturbed.

Nonetheless, there was a very bright spot in my life. In the fall of 1981, I had been showing my cat furniture at a show in Hamilton, Ohio, when Bonnie Luke walked by. Bonnie is a breeder from Indianapolis. In her arms that day was something I had never seen before: a little black Scottish Fold cat. The breed is named for its ears; they fold forward and lie across the top of the head.

As the story goes, a kitten with folded ears was first discovered in 1961 in Scotland among a litter of barn cats. A little white female, she was taken to a veterinarian who bred her with a British shorthair.

Bonnie's cat, an adorable little round-faced male, struck me as so unusual that I burst out laughing. When I stopped, I knew I had to have one.

Although Bonnie's cat was not available, she allowed him to take up temporary residence at my booth for the rest of the show. As an attention-getter, the cat would surely draw crowds and thereby increase cat furniture sales. People, after all, are accustomed to cats that flatten their ears as a sign of anger. This docile little fellow with his ears folded forward was bound to provoke comment.

At the Hamilton, Ohio, cat show, my convictions fell flat. Apparently tuckered out, Bonnie's cat spent all weekend dozing on my cat furniture. His head down, his body wound into a furry little ball, he could hardly be distinguished by his ears. Customers purchased cat houses. But the little black cat snoozed through every transaction.

Still, I wanted a Scottish Fold of my own. Awake, with its folded ears in full view, a Scottish Fold would make a pampered prop luxuriating across a cat house and mesmerizing customers.

Bonnie called months later. She had another Scottish Fold. This one, she assured me, was also mild mannered and well adjusted. I didn't have the nerve to ask about its sleeping patterns. I promised to take the cat sight unseen. The price was $300.

Mind you, my heart was set on another little black male. Instead, Bonnie showed me Tasha, a two-year-old faded-calico female. I was crestfallen. Had I not been a man of my word, I doubt that I would have taken her.

Expecting nothing, I put Tasha on a table, ready to size up my costly mistake. And then, as if on cue, Tasha rolled over. She wanted her tummy to be rubbed. I was smitten. I gave Bonnie the money and even threw in a couple of cat houses.

In my van Tasha jumped up on the dashboard. There, never out of my sight, she rode the whole way home. Back in Mundelein, I took Tasha to my shop, which was to be her new home. Instantly she scooted up on a piece of cat furniture. I was so happy I nearly purred. And best of all, Tasha's distinguished career as one of the most famous feline models ever to drape herself on a cat house was about to begin.

Before Tasha, I had never dreamed of taking a cat on the road to a cat show. With the van filled with tree-limb perches, Ed and I already had our hands full. But sure enough, a week after I acquired Tasha, she rode with the furniture to the Nashville Cat Fanciers show in Tennessee; Tasha stayed on the dashboard.

I brought her along because I had done my homework. Several days before the show, I telephoned the *Tennessean* newspaper. Still positive that the combination of one-of-a-kind cat furniture and a flop-eared feline would prove irresistible, I spoke to a reporter. It's very possible she thought I was pulling her leg. But if for no other reason than to satisfy her curiosity, she scheduled Tasha and me for an interview. Especially for the interview, I made a new cat house with an air conditioner/skylight, otherwise known as a planned hole in the roof.

At the newspaper offices, I jabbered. Tasha posed for the photographer, then hid behind a filing cabinet. The next day our story covered nearly half the features page. In a large photo, Tasha stood in the cat house like an invincible sentry, her head jutting from the roof, her left front paw draped possessively near the front door. CAT FANCIER BUILDS HOMES TO PLEASE FINICKY FELINES, the headline read.

Tasha and the cat house also made the local television news in Nashville.

Later Tasha and my expanding line of feline furniture would be featured in the *Pittsburgh Post Gazette*, the *Blade* in Toledo, Ohio, and the *St. Petersburg Times* in Florida.

Wordsmiths, it seemed, were having almost as good a time as I was. George Ney goes "out on a limb" to satisfy felines, reporters punned. My credo, according to United Press International, was "a cat's home should be its cat-sle." Ney gives new meaning to the term *cat house*, others wrote.

Naturally, I can't vouch that Tasha was dying to give new meaning to her own role as "pitchwoman" for a line of cat furniture. But I do know that despite stardom and notoriety, her sweet and laid-back nature has never changed.

I think Tasha was born a grandmother; as long as I've known her, she has had three speeds: slow, slow, and slow. When she is ready to be hugged, she is huggable. She is almost always lovable. Tasha is also perpetually calm and always ready to spend hours lolling on the cat furniture. The dark markings around her eyes give her an I'll-eat-you-alive glare. This, plus her full face and folded ears, have

Tasha (Photo by Bill Powers)

prompted some wags to call her Bulldog. I call her beautiful and terribly independent-minded.

Therefore, it seems all the more curious that part of Tasha's fame and much of the furniture's prominence traces to a male named Snoop. An amazing cat, Snoop belongs to Tom Drbal of Lincoln, Nebraska. I first met them at a cat show in Omaha, where Tasha and I were selling furniture.

Tom had taught Snoop to roll over and jump through a hoop. Showgoers were astonished. Most of us believed that cats, no matter how smart and devoted, were simply too stubborn to be trained.

But Snoop was a myth-buster. His ancestors were brilliant, I concluded, because they had fooled the rest of us into believing that cats couldn't be trained.

But now there was something I had to know: Could other cats—specifically Tasha—learn to do tricks?

Faster than a battered van, my mind was racing. If Tasha's merely standing in a cat house could cause her to become a media darling, what would happen if she had a repertoire of tricks?

Feigning confidence, I informed Tasha that she would soon become a sought-after performer. Mind you, I had never trained even a dog. But relying on instincts—my own—we began. My workbench became Tasha's makeshift stage.

Sitting down was "our" first trick. Because I could figure out no other way to begin, I put one hand under Tasha's chin and the other over her fanny. "Sit, Tasha, sit," I commanded. I said it over. And over. And over.

Gauging Tasha's progress was difficult. She jumped off the workbench. I put her back. She jumped off again. I retrieved her. What this taught me was to try to keep Tasha within arm's reach. I could trust her, but only as far as I could reach her.

Tasha also set me straight on feline attention spans. On the workbench she hardly ever gave me more than five minutes of her time. Often she would give less. To signal the end of a session, she would appear more bored and distracted than usual. Then she would jump off the workbench and disappear into the shop. An hour later, if I could find her, she might allow me another five minutes of training time.

Not wishing to infringe on Tom's territory, I never questioned him about technique. Besides, if Tasha proved an apt pupil, I was sure the country was big enough for more than one trained cat.

Days after our training sessions began, Tasha actually sat. And then she advanced to the point where she sat not only when I tapped her fanny but often when I simply told her to. I was ecstatic. Tasha seemed fairly neutral about the whole thing.

But could she learn more? Or had she/we reached our limits? Lying down was a logical next trick to attempt. I put two fingers on Tasha's shoulder blades and pushed gently. She was reluctant. She was bored. But after three days of practice, Tasha lay down all by herself.

The actual maneuver, I'm sure, left her unfazed. But judging by the number of times she rolled over for her tummy to be rubbed, I could tell she appreciated the extra petting and attention. Cats, like people, respond to love and affection.

Next came rolling over. Tasha needed incentive. For motivation, I supplied several morsels of her favorite food. Starting with Tasha in the lie-down position, I would move a treat across her nose (so she could catch the scent) and toward her shoulder. If and when she rolled over, I gave her the treat.

It took us a full week—five minutes an hour for as many hours as we could squeeze into a day. But Tasha learned to roll to one side and then the other, and all for the same morsel of treat.

Soon we were ready for begging. I put Tasha in a sitting position. To entice her to lift her front paws, I held out a treat. To get the treat, Tasha had to lift her body. Each day I raised the treat a bit higher. One day Tasha went all the way up on her hind legs.

To complete her salesmanship course, Tasha needed to thank her customers. A handshake—although I had never seen a cat give one—seemed appropriate.

At first I was stumped. I softly tapped the inside of Tasha's front leg. To make me stop, I thought she'd raise her paw.

But Tasha was too smart for that. I tapped; she turned and walked away. This continued for days. But ultimately Tasha became bothered enough by the tapping to lift her paw. I extended my hand. It was our first paw-shake.

Whenever customers wandered into Cat House Originals, I couldn't resist putting Tasha through her paces. Mostly she obliged. People were amazed. Sometimes they left still carrying on about "that marvelous cat."

Meanwhile, there was something I had to know. Beyond the ruckus of my shop, would Tasha perform?

In search of a receptive and not overly critical audience, I volunteered our services at the Brentwood North Nursing and Rehabilitation Center in Riverwoods, Illinois. To increase Tasha's sense of security, and probably mine too, I brought along a piece of cat furniture.

During the show there were times when I had to coax and recoax Tasha. More than once she balked, showing every sign of refusing to do a trick. "Tasha, you're making me look bad," I said with a laugh. Tasha just stood there.

"Ladies and gentlemen, you didn't actually believe a cat could perform, now did you?" I said only half teasingly. If I just talked long enough, I prayed, Tasha might do something.

Finally, to her everlasting credit, she did. She eventually executed each of her tricks, then hopped up on her cat furniture. The seniors adored her. We have returned often to the Riverwoods center.

In time I increased Tasha's repertoire to eighteen tricks. She learned to jump through a hoop, play a toy piano (the trick here was not plunking the keys, but learning to tolerate the noise), roll a barrel, ride in a baby stroller, and sit in one of my homemade carpet-covered high chairs.

One day I got a call from Al Hall, executive producer of WGN-TV's "Bozo Show" in Chicago. Al wanted Tasha to be a guest. "The Bozo Show," starring a costumed clown, is picked up by stations across the country.

The day of the taping, the host had just one reservation. With all the moms and young children in the audience, he feared it would be improper to mention cat houses.

Moments later, Tasha and I went on camera. She delighted the kids in the studio, really hamming it up and doing half a dozen tricks. Between stunts, the host called attention to her cat condos.

Back in Mundelein, I was experiencing growing pains. In need of display space, I exhibited cat furniture in the parking lot at my shop. The mayor objected, saying this didn't quite conform with Mundelein regulations.

Not long afterward, I relocated to nearby Ivanhoe, Illinois. Again there were problems. My building showed considerable wear and tear; the landlord would commit himself to virtually no fix-up work.

Disgruntled, I moved several miles farther out to a small shopping center in Wauconda, Illinois. That's where I've stayed.

As usual, my shop is nothing fancy. It's a workshop, but this time with a display window.

Ed Zerr is still building cat furniture. Debbie Burnett, who takes full credit for persuading me to carpet the cat houses in colors other than brown and beige, has become Cat House Originals' upholsterer and girl Friday.

For a time animal lover and friend Charlene Whitney came to work to organize my files. For years I've stored newspaper clippings, plus odds and ends, in cardboard boxes. The boxes in turn are stored on the floor, the chair, the desk, and the table.

Charlene gave up on alphabetizing my clutter. Instead, she assembled cat houses and the most unforgettable cat house parade float I've ever been part of. Wauconda was scheduled to have a big procession not long after Cat House Originals came to town. To support Wauconda and to introduce residents to the cat houses, Charlene insisted that we participate.

Onto a little red wagon she strapped a gigantic piece of cat furniture. The cat house was so unwieldy that it took two husky teenagers to balance it, and even then it tottered. Another teen, also husky, pulled the wagon.

Charlene and her two children—outfitted as bewhiskered cats, complete with tails—scampered down the street. My assignment was to wheel a baby stroller full of cats; this was the trick I first taught Tasha. Leading all of us was Angel, Charlene's Sheltie show dog. Angel pranced, jumped through a hoop, rolled over, and picked up a basket.

And just in case anyone had missed the cat furniture, still teetering in the little red wagon, Charlene found a couple of kids to blanket the crowd with promotional pamphlets.

Suffice it to say, people knew that Cat House Originals had rolled into town.

My life with Tasha and the cat furniture has been further complicated and enriched by my fairly regular acquisition of cats. Somehow I never go looking for more cats. But through a friend, a friend of a friend, or a humane society, I seem forever to be adding tenants to my cat houses.

After Tasha came Miss Hiss, Madame Tanya (every cat house needs a madame), Valentine, Peanut Butter I, Scupa (Self-Contained Uninhibited Purring Apparatus), Spooker, Victoria, and Peanut Butter II.

Madame Tanya and Peanut Butter I and II are Scottish Folds; the rest are "purr alleys." Adapting the methods I pioneered with Tasha, I taught each cat nearly a dozen tricks.

As a furry feline ensemble, they're members of the cat chorus line and subjects of Queen Hiss. Kitty chorines, they sit all in a row, their tails sometimes thumping. In a sequence called the Queen and Her Court, Miss Hiss sits haughtily in her high chair/throne while her Cat Guards, mostly obedient, stand nearby.

With a couple of cats at a time, plus a van of cat furniture, I continue to appear at the country's cat shows. Many times the cats have been featured on television and radio and in newspapers; given a chance, I always mention the cat houses, too.

Tasha was the 1985 promotion cat for the American Veterinary Medical Association's National Pet Week. Oscar was in a Chevrolet commercial with legendary football star Dick Butkus, formerly of the Chicago Bears.

The other cats have starred in commercials and industrial tapes for plate glass, cough syrup, and insurance. More-

Queen Hiss and her courtiers (Photo by Fred Stevenson)

over, they have been featured in *Cats, Cat Fancy* and *The Cat Fancy Almanac* magazines. Along with me, they sometimes co-host my TV show, "All About Animals," a public-access program for Highwood, Illinois.

But it's a funny thing about performing cats. No matter how celebrated, cats are still cats. When we're not on the road, we're back at the shop in Wauconda; the cats have the run of the place. But there's no spot they'd rather be than on whatever cat houses happen to be on the floor that day. From a carpeted perch or tunnel, anchored to a tree limb, they happily doze, play, and watch the world go by.

4
Starting Cat House Building

King Solomon stabled his horses. Pigs are penned. And for the Fidos of the world, there have always been doghouses. But when it comes to personalized quarters, domesticated cats have long come up on the short end.

Perhaps we've been cowed by the pussycat's reputation. After all, how dare we second-guess an animal so notoriously independent-minded that until recently cats bamboozled us into believing they couldn't sit on command, roll over, or play dead? (See my first book, *The Educated Cat: How to Teach Your Cat to Do Tricks*, 1987, also published by E. P. Dutton.)

Until now, and really because most of us didn't know any better, we have attempted to satisfy feline wants in the most human ways. First, cats doze an estimated 65 percent of the time. If a human spent the bulk of his life reposing, he would deserve no less than a grandiose bed, we've concluded. Therefore, our well-intentioned gifts to cats have included itty-bitty kitty canopy beds and itty-bitty kitty mattresses.

Second, house cats require shelter. Again, doing our human level best, we've nailed a roof—namely ours—over felines' heads. Lastly, cats scratch. Initially we were stymied by this need; human beings who repeatedly engaged in such a behavior would be called on the carpet for sure. But eventually we mass-produced our notion of what an indoor scratching post should be—a carpeted two-by-four or four-by-four.

Some of the earliest scratching posts bore most strongly our misdirected human imprint. Resembling nothing so much as floor-to-ceiling pole lamps, the posts were made of carpeted plywood and held in place at the top by a spring. Unfortunately springs sometimes sprang, and rickety posts would then clatter down. Terrified by such an experience, some cats would henceforth avoid scratching posts altogether, and attack with renewed vigor all chair and table legs.

BUILT-IN APPEAL

The cat houses you are about to build are different indeed. They are predicated on specifically satisfying feline needs— a pause that refreshes, security, and the proper height, contours, and carpeting. Secondarily, the cat house designs are intended to charm the socks off cat-loving humans.

This combination seems to be unbeatable. Most felines have a sixth sense about these houses; the cats know they're theirs.

Many times when I deliver cat houses to customers, the cats don't even wait until we humans decide at what angle a cat house might look best in a particular room. As soon as I step in the door, the cats are all over the cat houses.

To skeptics, I sometimes mention that a spritz of catnip spray could possibly increase a cat house's appeal. But to tell the truth, I've never found it necessary.

AGE OF CAT HOUSE OCCUPANTS

Cats are never too young or too old for a cat house. When kittens are about six weeks old, they're ready for a unit with a tunnel on the bottom. The tunnels, which are made of sturdy paperboard tubing covered by carpet, sit on a carpeted plywood base. From the floor, the tunnels measure just about ten inches tall.

A favorite kitty parlor game is for one or more kittens to be on top of the tunnel as their litter mates crawl through. When crawlers emerge, they are attacked by the Top of the Tunnel Gang. After numerous rounds, players sometimes change positions.

Kittens do not require special kitty houses, unless of course you'd like to build one. As a rule, kittens prefer the Tunnel of Love or any unit with a tunnel on the bottom. Until the kittens get older, they pretty much ignore the carpeted components near the top of many cat houses; these they'll grow into.

Adolescent felines, those from about eight months to two years old, relish height, and therefore are particularly fond of cat houses with perches, tubes, and little houses—in stepladder fashion—all the way to the top of a tree-limb scratching post. As a cat lover and a do-it-yourselfer, you will know how far your cat can safely leap in a single bound. Space the cat house components accordingly.

Older cats, like the rest of us, tend to slow down. Tender Vittles, the cat with arthritis, is no exception. For mature felines, the most appropriate cat houses are generally the floor models, and the units with perches just a foot or two from the ground. Floor models include the Royal Cat-sle, the Catnip Saloon, the Southern Plantation House for Aristocats, the World War I Biplane, and the Kitty Choo-Choo.

TERRITORIAL RIGHTS

Will four cats share one cat house? Will three Kitty Tree Houses in one human house be enough, or too much? Will two cats demand separate cat houses in separate rooms? These decisions are not ours to make. But as soon as you build your first units, you'll speedily have your answers.

Naturally, if you have more than one cat and you're hoping for joint occupancy, hope for the best; go for some of the larger, multiperch units. That's what Janet Fink did. Janet is the co-owner with Pat Russell of the Catnip Shoppe in Long Grove, Illinois. Janet has eight cats and two large Kitty Tree Houses.

Until recently she also had Bonnie. Bonnie was a "tuxedo cat" with four white paws, a white chest, and a fervid attachment to a little carpeted house on one of the tree houses. The eldest of Janet's cats, Bonnie was quite willing to share the tree houses with the other cats. But the carpeted house was hers. Period.

Even after Bonnie died, her keep-your-paws-off edict still prevailed. "I would put the other cats in the carpeted house, and they'd jump out," Janet said.

"Bonnie weighed fifteen pounds. I don't know if it was out of fear or respect for her, but for the longest time after her death, the others would not use her house."

This same sense of possessiveness, coupled with resistance to change, may also extend to the relocation of a cat house or the acquisition of a new one. Creatures of habit, some cats are at least mildly traumatized when their cat houses are moved, even to another room. Minimize feline anxiety. If you move a cat house, always try to relocate it near a window. The mouth-watering sight of an outdoor bird in flight has been known to perk up even the most woebegone felines.

STABILITY

Regardless of which cat houses you build, stability is of prime importance. Whenever indicated in the directions, use sinker nails, which are known for their holding power. To attach a tree limb to a plywood base, you will use six 20-penny sinker nails. For maximum stability, four sinkers are hammered through the plywood and into the outer perimeter of the limb; the remaining two are driven into the center of the limb.

To nail perches and tunnels to tree limbs, 16-penny sinker nails are recommended. And any time any part of a cat house seems the least bit wobbly, add more nails or brace the unit with additional tree limbs. These bracing limbs can reach upward from the base to the top of the unit, or from a platform to a perch. Should a finished unit ever seem top-heavy, compensate by laying down a short limb on the base; hammer it in place. Cats won't mind a bit; to them, it's another scratching post.

Whenever platforms are used on some of the heavier units, such as the Cat Condo, the directions call for notching limbs with a saw so that platforms will slip easily and securely into tree limbs.

CONVERSATION PIECES

No two tree limbs are alike, so every cat house you build will be one of a kind. Expect it also to be a conversation piece. To Donna Dunlap, partner in the Park View Pet Shop in Chicago, my condos and perches "look like something out of a Dr. Seuss children's story. They're fairy-tale houses."

Among her clients, Donna counts an avid art collector whose home is filled with often pricey sculptures. In such an environment, she says, a George Ney cat house becomes yet another "work of art. It becomes indistinguishable" from the other pieces.

Pattie Cantella of suburban Chicago tells a similar story.

Pattie has five cats and five of my cat houses. One evening a friend dropped by. In one corner of her condominium he noticed something looming. "Are you into modern art?" he asked.

"No, I'm into cat furniture!" she replied.

CAT HOUSE/YOUR HOUSE MAINTENANCE

Whether your cat furniture looms over everything or follows a more minimalist tradition—short limbs and low perches—is your decision. But just remember, the larger and more exuberant your cat or cats, the more likely their cat houses will need occasional tightening. Add nails as necessary.

And each time consider how much easier and cheaper it is to repair the cat's house than to repair whatever the cat might have done to your house, provided he hadn't done it to his first.

To clean a cat house, just remove the cat hair. Use a hand-held vacuum sweeper, a wire brush, or a fine-tooth comb.

Certainly, having a cat house is no guarantee that felines will never again swat your hanging lamp or paw your furniture. But when cats have cat houses, many seem to prefer their own perches and tunnels, at least part of the day.

Cupcake, a black cat with a white mustache, tummy, and paws, is a little devil. But at night, when she isn't unwinding the toilet paper, hiding the bathtub plug, or batting on the faucet and scooting into the bathtub, Charlene Whitney almost always knows where to find her: Cupcake will be in the bedroom, asleep in her blue-carpeted cat house.

Under normal circumstances, a regularly maintained cat house can last for years. Still, there can be exceptions. Hazel Gellinger, a cat breeder in Northlake, Illinois, sometimes has ten to twenty cats at a time. To date, she has had six cat houses; almost once a year, she orders a new one.

"I have to," she says. "The cats wear them out. They

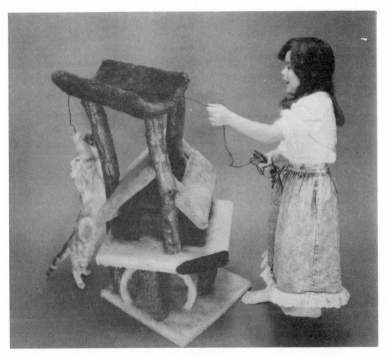

Kerri Smith and Peanut Butter enjoying a perch.

claw, sleep, play tag, and just goof off in the cat houses. But the cats don't seem to bother my own furniture at all; I really think it's because they have something of their own."

SELECTION OF TREE LIMBS

Because the tree limbs on a cat house will become your cat's approved indoor scratching posts, select with care. Choose wood that is soft enough for the cat to claw. The best wood, I find, is willow, followed by birch, cottonwood, and a soft maple. Leave the bark intact.

Use interestingly shaped limbs. The more crooks, bends, and curves in the limbs, the more intriguing your final product will be. All the diagrams and photographs that follow are meant to be a catalyst. Be guided by your imagination and your tree limbs.

Frequently I will refer to the *principal* tree limb in a cat house, and to other limbs that brace or support a unit. All major components of the cat house will be hammered to the principal limb; it is most often the first limb attached to a base. Toward the end of construction, support limbs are added to lend further stability.

Cats are attracted to limbs by the aroma of the wood. For humans, the scent is no stronger than having a log sitting near the fireplace.

And this brings up another point. Do not substitute already cut firewood for the limbs in cat houses. Most likely the firewood will be too short, and won't be as serviceable for your pet.

Watch your cat the next time it claws its scratching post or itches its paws. Cats stretch all the way up on their hind legs. This is how felines should be able to use tree-limb scratching posts. A short chunk of firewood just won't do much good.

Tree limbs at the base of a cat house should measure about four to seven inches in diameter. This will lend stability. As these same limbs taper off (the portion of the principal limb at the top of the cat house), a diameter at the tip of two or so inches is perfectly acceptable; a little thicker is fine, too.

You may be lucky enough to have an unlimited supply of tree limbs growing in your own backyard or in a nearby woods. But if you take a limb from the ground, make sure it doesn't appear to have been there for years as a five-star hangout for bugs.

NO PESTICIDES

Do not treat the limbs with chemicals or pesticides. This is unnecessary and may keep cats away or could possibly harm them.

After thousands of cat houses, I have received just one complaint about bugs. I still remember the culprit limb. It's one I found in a forest, at the foot of a tree. Although it appeared to be firm and clean, it was not. I immediately disposed of the cat house and gave the buyer her money back.

Additional sources of tree limbs include tree trimmers, who may be quite willing to sell or otherwise part with a few specimens, and foremen and contractors at construction sites. Ask before carting anything away.

At the construction site, also check the pile of cast-off wood. From throwaways, you may find enough plywood to build a whole cat house. Plywood will be used for the base of the cat house, for platforms, and possibly for perches. One-inch plywood is preferable, especially for bases and platforms. But half-inch and three-quarter-inch plywood can be used for some cat house components.

Naturally, wood that can't be found or otherwise scrounged up can always be purchased. Although I must say, before I needed large quantities of supplies, it always delighted me to know I could earn money by using scraps and remnants that others were throwing away.

BUILDER'S TUBING

Plywood can be used for perches and tunnels. But I find that cats are lots happier with cat houses when builder's tubing is used for these structures. The round tubing conforms more closely than plywood to the cat's own contours.

Builder's tubing is used mainly for pouring concrete for columns and foundations. The tubing is made in different diameters and can be cut into the desired length to make the forms for pouring. It is manufactured by various companies under such trade names as Sonotube® Fibre Forms,* Handiform Perma Tubes, and Crown Fibre Forms. The tubing is sold at retail by lumber companies and other dealers in building supplies.

The most widely available make, in my own experience,

* Sonotube is a registered trademark of the Sonoco Products Company, Hartsville, South Carolina.

is the Sonotube form, produced by the Sonoco Products Company in Hartsville, South Carolina. For convenience, in my directions for building cat houses I will refer to them as Sonotubes, as they are popularly called. Other makes can also be used if your local dealer has them in the needed dimensions.

Sonotubes are made of tough, multiple-ply paperboard, much stronger than cardboard. You will need tubing that measures twelve inches in diameter. In this size, Sonotubes are approximately one-fourth inch thick. This would be too thin for larger cats. The instructions in this book therefore include directions for doubling the thickness by gluing or stapling one one-fourth inch layer inside another to attain the desired thickness of one-half inch.

If you have any trouble finding tubing in your area, you may telephone the Sonoco Products Company at Hartsville for information on the closest distributor of Sonotubes. The telephone number is 803-383-7000.

Sonotubes are generally sold in lengths of twelve feet or more. This may sound like a lifetime supply, but keep in mind that if your tubing is one-fourth inch thick, you will be using a double thickness. If a completed perch measures twelve or eighteen inches long, it contains twenty-four or thirty-six inches of tubing, respectively.

Some larger cat houses, such as the Southern Plantation House, use ten feet of tubing. If you're making more than one cat house for yourself or are making one for your feline and one for a local humane society or your favorite veterinarian, the twelve feet should not go to waste. Most dealers will be glad to cut the tubing into pieces small enough to fit into your car, but check the perch dimensions specified before anyone does any cutting.

Prices for Sonotubes and other makes of tubing vary slightly in different areas of the country, but generally do not exceed $2.00 or $2.50 per foot. For twelve feet, which would be more than ample tubing for most houses, the tubing shouldn't cost more than $25 or $30. If you were to buy a

A Tunnel of Love made from a Sonotube

completed cat house from a pet shop or at a cat show, prices of $150, $200, and up are not unusual for larger units.

CARPETING

You'll be carpeting all cat house surfaces except the tree limbs and the bottom of the base. It's usually also unnecessary to carpet the bottom of the platform used to support the sloping-roofed houses, the Catnip Saloon, and some of the other structures. The bottom of the platform will not be used by the cat; if it isn't visible to you when you position the platform on your principal tree limbs, save the carpeting.

Color-wise, some people favor neutral carpeting so a cat house can blend into many rooms. Others prefer using a leftover swatch of their own carpeting for a result so customized that it might have been commissioned by a top-dog designer. Another advantage to using your own carpeting is that you've already paid for it once; it will cost you nothing extra to use it on a cat house.

For contrast, on some cat houses I use one color carpet to trim the edges of the base and the perches, and another color for their interiors. Another option is to trim a perch in the same color used for the interior of the base, and trim the base in the same carpeting used for the interior of the perch.

The amount of carpet necessary for each cat house is listed with each unit. Amounts vary from a two-foot square for a simple Scratching Post to a piece of carpeting twelve feet by seven feet for a well-fortified Royal Cat-sle or a sweet Gingerbread House.

If you're able to scrounge up small remnants on your own, combine two, three, or more of them to reach the total amount of carpet necessary for a particular unit.

Otherwise, carpet remnants are widely available through carpet stores, and often through carpet layers. Shop around for the best price. Furthermore, if you happen to know someone who is about to recarpet, ask for some of his or her discards. No matter how long rugs have been down, carpet that has been under a bed or couch is usually going to look brand new.

For a more professional-looking final product, I recommend carpeting all plywood pieces and paperboard tubes before hammering the cat house together. The one exception, as noted in the directions for the individual houses, is the roof of some units, which is carpeted after assembly and helps to reinforce the whole unit.

From my years of experience in the carpet and tile business, I would suggest that you upholster a piece by first draping it with a somewhat-larger-than-necessary piece of carpet. Then use heavy-duty staples, tacks, glue, or cement to attach the carpet to the piece. With a razor-blade knife, trim away the excess carpet.

Tree limbs will not wear out, but should the carpeting on your tabby's house begin to look shabby, you have a choice. Either recover the worn-out piece or build a new cat house.

You're ready to begin. In the next two chapters you will find photographs and construction diagrams for a wide variety of cat houses. We will start with the more simple units and then, using the same basic construction techniques, progress to the more elaborate models.

5
A Cat's Home Is Its Cat-sle

There are many ways to satisfy a cat's as yet largely unmet needs for personalized living and scratching quarters. But there is no simpler way to do your cat and your furniture a favor than by building a scratching post.

SCRATCHING POST

CARPET DIMENSIONS REQUIRED: 2 feet by 2 feet

To purchase a decent scratching post, you'll easily spend $15 or more. As a resourceful do-it-yourselfer, you can whittle costs down considerably.

The base of the Scratching Post is an 18-inch plywood square 1 inch thick. After experimenting with various di-

Scratching Post

mensions, I find these measurements to be ideal. The resulting base will be large and durable enough to firmly anchor the post you'll soon be attaching, but small enough to slip unobtrusively near a window or elsewhere in a room.

Carpet the top and sides of the base.

Chop down, scavenge, or otherwise procure a section of tree limb 4 to 6 inches in diameter and 18 to 24 inches long. Be guided by the shape of your limb, but to make the limb more manageable during subsequent construction steps, cut the limb straight across the bottom. If the limb curves, you can angle the limb and still make a straight cut across the bottom. On most of the units that follow, you will also be leveling the tops of the limbs so they can be anchored firmly to perches and other components. On the scratching post, either level the top of the limb or let it naturally taper off. The recommended diameter of limb will add stability.

However, if your tranquility is rocked by indoor tree limbs of any diameter, if limbs seem too rustic, or if plywood is more accessible, you may substitute two-by-fours or four-by-fours. Either use one four-by-four, cut 18 to 24 inches long, or nail together two two-by-fours.

It has been my experience that cats much prefer tree limbs to plywood. But many of my competitors continue to use two-by-fours and four-by-fours and claim their kitty clients are satisfied.

If you're using a tree limb, leave it intact, with the bark on. Otherwise, carpet the sides and top of the four-by-four or two two-by-fours.

Another alternative is to skip the carpet altogether and wrap the four-by-four from top to bottom with a clothesline. Keep the rope in place by tying or nailing down the ends. A tightly woven rope will be squishy enough for a cat to dig into it, claw it, or rub its paws against it, but usually not so squishy that the cat can get caught or tangled.

To attach the post to the center of the carpeted base, use six 20-penny sinker nails. Invert the structures so the base is on top of the post. Drive in four nails as close as possible to the edge of the post. If you're using a four-by-four or two two-by-fours instead of a tree limb, aim one nail in each of the four corners. With either the tree limb or the lumber, drive the remaining two nails into the center.

Show the cat your handiwork. Let nature take its course.

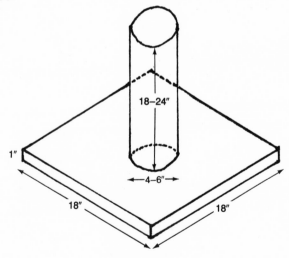

Scratching Post

DELUXE SCRATCH PAD

CARPET DIMENSIONS REQUIRED: 5 feet by 2 feet
SONOTUBE: 18 inches

A Scratching Post is strictly for scratching. But a Deluxe
Scratch Pad is so-o-o-o much more. Not only will your
felines scratch and squirm, but with a carpeted perch they
gain an observation deck. So do you.

Wait till you see the cats playing and dozing on the
perch. The Deluxe Scratch Pad is well worth the extra effort.
Tasha sleeps in a semicircle. I say "semi" because only half of
her is on the perch. The rest—her fanny—hangs down.
Scupa has his own snooze style. His head and front paws
droop off the perch; the rest of him stays on it.

To create a feline sleep/play station, build a Scratching

Deluxe Scratch Pad with a
carpeted plywood top

*Deluxe Scratch Pad with a
top made from a tube*

Post exactly as described in the previous section. To make a perch on top, you have a choice. Either use builder's tubing, which I recommend because of its contours, or select a piece of plywood. If you are using plywood, you will need a 16-inch square.

Carpet the top and sides of the plywood.

If you are using Sonotube, start with 18 inches of 12-inch-diameter tubing. With a soft or flexible tape measure, measure along the rim of the tubing, from the inside (this would be the circumference of the circle). Mark off three sections of approximately 12½ inches apiece. Saw them lengthwise so they remain 18 inches long. Put one section inside another to yield a perch that is ½ inch thick. Staple, tack, cement, or glue these two sections of paperboard tubing together. Save the remaining section for another cat house. Carpet the perch.

As for carpet, you're limited only by your imagination.

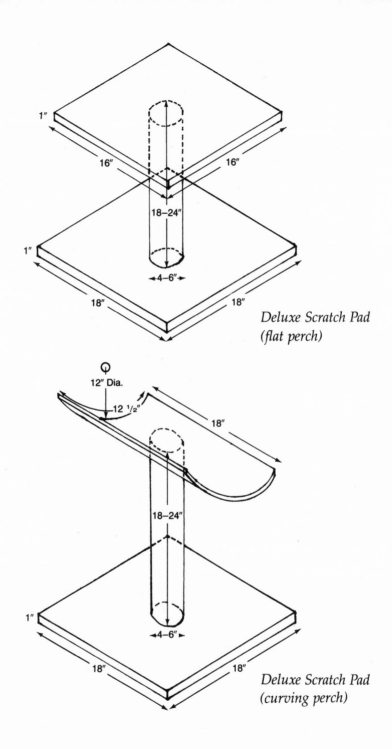

1″

16″   16″

18–24″

4–6″

1″

18″   18″

Deluxe Scratch Pad
(flat perch)

12″ Dia.

12 ½″   18″

18–24″

4–6″

1″

18″   18″

Deluxe Scratch Pad
(curving perch)

Jean Farmer of Bloomington, Indiana, suggests that perches can highlight a cat's breeding, almost like a coat of arms. For example, a Persian-carpet perch would befit a Persian cat. Short of the real thing, you can often buy a pseudo-Persian carpet about the size of a large doormat. Use it to cover your perch. If what remains is too small for the base, cover the latter in a solid color, opting for one that has been used in the Persian design.

Carefully center the scratching post under the carpeted perch. If you are using a tree limb, be sure to level it across the top so it can be firmly secured to the perch. However, be guided by the limb. Determine the most interesting angle for leveling the top.

Ever since I went into the cat furniture business full-time in 1980, I've been manufacturing these deluxe units in my shop. The Deluxe Scratch Pad remains one of my steadiest sellers. It's a feline-pleaser, and consequently a favorite with humans.

Up the Wall

UP THE WALL

CARPET DIMENSIONS REQUIRED: 1 foot by 3 feet

Let's face it. Certain habits, even in those we love most dearly, can drive us bananas. Here's a possible precaution. So that your cat's scratching against the woodwork does not send you up the wall, reach for plywood, carpeting, and a tree limb.

This economical little wall saver is also a space saver. Measuring just 11 inches deep, it is tailor-made for apartment dwellers and those whose homes have limited floor and walk space. Start with two pieces of plywood. The one that will rest directly against the wall should be 12 inches wide and 24 inches high. The base is 12 inches wide and 11 inches long. Carpet both pieces.

Form a 90-degree angle with the plywood by nailing one of the 12-inch sides of the base to one of the 12-inch edges of the longer piece.

From a tree limb about 3 to 4 inches in diameter, cut a 24-inch section. This section of the limb will be a combination scratching post and brace. Position the limb near one of the corners of the base. Lean the limb against the larger piece of plywood. Use four 16-penny sinker nails to attach the base to the limb. Use two 16-penny sinkers to anchor the top of the limb to the larger piece of plywood.

Position the unit against the wall. Whoever said anything about bananas?

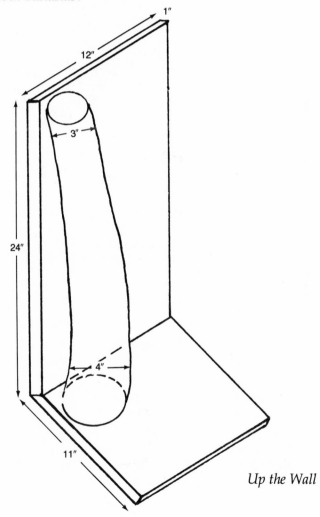

Up the Wall

*Tunnel of Love with one
perch*

TUNNEL OF LOVE

CARPET DIMENSIONS REQUIRED: 5 feet by 2 feet, or 6 feet by 2
   feet, depending on the perch style you select
SONOTUBE: up to 3½ feet

Cats not only feel comfy with a perch under their tummies
but often seem to feel secure inside a tunnel.

   I learned this indirectly from a dog lover. He came to me
with a Sonotube measuring 18 inches in diameter and a
request for an indoor doghouse. I mounted the tube on a
piece of plywood, did some cutting and carpeting, and
produced something he claimed drew raves from his Rover.

   At this point I was making cat house perches strictly out
of plywood. But thinking I might be able to incorporate
small tubes into some of the cat furniture, I brought some
Sonotube measuring 12 inches in diameter into my shop.

There it sat one day while I was out making deliveries. When I returned, an employee, Joseph Hoffmeier—a friend of my younger daughter, Cheryl—presented me with a brand-new unit. To a Deluxe Scratch Pad with a plywood perch, he had added a carpeted tunnel. I sensed at once that we had a winner.

The Tunnel of Love appeals to cats of all ages, including kittens. Many times I've watched kittens playfully batting each other in and on the tunnel.

The plywood base measures 20 inches by 20 inches. Carpet the top and sides.

At a diagonal on the base, you will attach a 12-inch-long tunnel. The tunnel can be constructed of builder's tubing or plywood.

To make a tunnel from Sonotube, start with a 24-inch-long piece of tubing measuring 12 inches in diameter. The Sonotube is approximately ¼ inch thick. To reach a cat-tested, desirable thickness of ½ inch, make a vertical cut with your saw so you are left with two 12-inch-long tubes, each having a diameter of 12 inches.

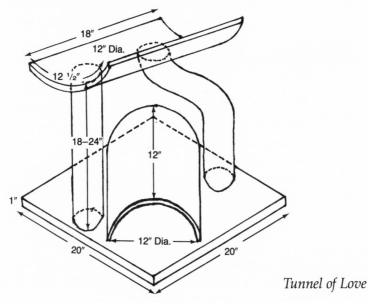

Tunnel of Love

Tunnel of Love with a
square tunnel

From one of the tubes, saw off a strip 1 inch wide and 12 inches long. Slide this tube into the other tube. You now have an overall tube thickness of ½ inch. Glue, tack, staple, or cement the tubes together.

On the inside of the tube you have just assembled, take a tape measure, and along the rim (this would be the circumference of your tube's circle) mark off a 12½-inch section. Saw away this section, which will be 12½ inches wide and 12 inches long. Save this section for a perch/stepping-stone on one of your own customized units.

The larger section of your tubing is a tunnel big enough for even the heftiest of house cats to be able to crawl inside. Carpet the tunnel inside and out.

Rather than using tubing, you can also make a squared-off tunnel with plywood; you will need three pieces. The two sides of the tunnel measure 12 inches long and 9 inches high. The top is 12 inches by 12 inches. Nail the pieces together. Carpet the tunnel inside and out.

Take a tree limb 18 to 24 inches long, with one end measuring 4 to 6 inches in diameter. This is your principal limb. The large end will be positioned near one corner of your plywood base. But first, so the limb will sit solidly on the base, saw the bottom of the limb straight across. Or if you prefer, saw it straight across, but at an angle.

Turn the plywood base on its side. Holding the limb where you'd like it to be stationed, drive one 20-penny sinker nail through the plywood base and into the center of the limb. More nails will be added later.

Put the base upright. Adjust the tree limb until it looks right to you; for once, since a tree limb is a cat's natural scratching post, pleasing your feline will be no problem. Once you've determined the proper angle for the limb, turn the base back on its side and pound five more 20-penny nails into the tree limb.

Next you will attach the tunnel to the principal limb.

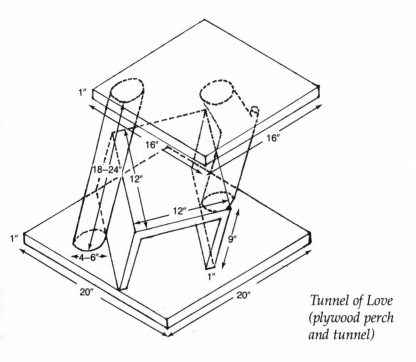

Tunnel of Love
(plywood perch
and tunnel)

Place the tunnel on a diagonal on the base, with the open ends of tunnel each facing a corner of the base. Slide one side of the tunnel against the limb. Hammer one 16-penny nail from the inside of the tunnel into the tree limb. More nails will be added later.

Level the top of the tree limb with your saw. This is where the cat's perch will sit. Again you have a choice: a perch made of tubing, which I find to be ideally sculpted for the cat's body, or a plywood perch.

The plywood perch is a 16-inch square. Carpet it.

For the curved perch, begin with 18 inches of Sonotube. Measuring from the inside and along the circumference, mark off three 12½-inch sections. Saw them lengthwise. Put one section inside another to make an 18-inch-long perch. Save the remaining section for half of another cat house perch.

Using a 16-penny sinker nail, hammer the perch (naturally, if it's the Sonotube perch, make sure it's in a concave position) to the top of the tree limb.

Next measure from the top of the base to the bottom of the perch. This will be the length of the second, or support, limb. Level both ends of the support limb with your saw. Using a 16-penny nail, attach the perch to the second tree limb.

Turn the base back on its side and nail six 20-penny nails into the bottom of the second tree limb.

Turn the base upright and use a 16-penny nail to attach the tunnel to the second tree limb.

Add more nails for reinforcement.

The Tunnel of Love is especially cozy for a whole cat family. So cozy, in fact, that you might opt for two larger models—the Deluxe Tunnel of Love with two perches and the Super Deluxe with three. Make more perches according to the directions already given. Then make just a few adjustments in the construction process. To accommodate the additional perches, your tree limbs will need to be somewhat longer. For a two-perch Deluxe Tunnel of Love, start

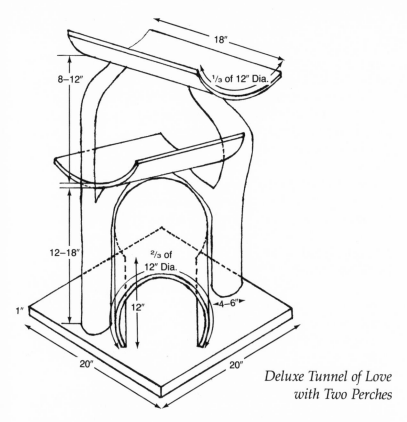

18"

8–12"

1/3 of 12" Dia.

12–18"

2/3 of
12" Dia.

1"

12"

4–6"

20"

20"

*Deluxe Tunnel of Love
with Two Perches*

with two tree limbs, still 4 to 6 inches in diameter, but now about 20 to 30 inches long. For the three-perch Super Deluxe unit, tree limbs should measure approximately 28 to 42 inches long; they remain 4 to 6 inches in diameter.

If your cats are already enjoying their one-perch Tunnel of Love, resist the temptation to add short limbs and another perch or perches to the existing unit. Cat houses must be sturdy. A key to their stability is the fact that one or more principal tree limbs span from the base to the uppermost component. A short limb nailed to a principal limb will undermine a cat house's stability.

Also, in building the two- and three-perch versions, shift the position of your tree limbs. Instead of resting under the first carpeted limb, as they do in the one-perch Tunnel of Love, the limbs will now be attached to the outside of the bottom perch. Use 16-penny sinker nails.

If you are building the two-perch unit, level the top of the limbs so they rest under the top perch. The distance between perches should be roughly 8 to 12 inches.

On a three-perch unit, the principal limbs will come along the sides of both the bottom perch and the middle perch. The principal limbs should then be leveled so they can be attached to the bottom of the top perch; for your cat's enjoyment and safety, the distance from the middle perch to the top perch should be approximately 8 to 12 inches. Use 16-penny sinker nails to anchor perches to limbs.

Two-Perch Deluxe
Tunnel of Love

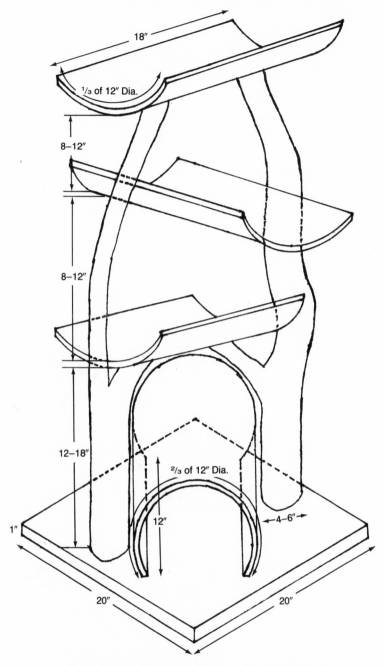

Super Deluxe Tunnel of Love with Three Perches

In these cat houses, as in all others, be guided by your limbs. Often you can incorporate their twists and curves. As in the accompanying diagrams for the larger Tunnels of Love, you may be able to find two limbs that branch off. Then one portion of each branch becomes one of your principal limbs, and the other portion is trimmed to come under the first perch, as a supporting limb.

Moreover, depending on the curve of the limbs, it may be possible to vary the angles of the perches; perhaps one or two can be parallel to the base and another can be positioned diagonally.

Three-Perch Super Deluxe Tunnel of Love

SKYLIGHT OVER KITTY LAND

CARPET DIMENSIONS REQUIRED: 12 feet by 6 feet
SONOTUBE: approximately 7 feet

This snazzy little number is so named for a cutout, or sky-light, which in feline terminology means an easy access/escape route. The cat house has three primary components: a tunnel, a full circle (the whole Sonotube) with a cutout, and a cat perch.

During a recent trip to Bloomington, Indiana, I delivered a white-carpeted Skylight over Kitty Land to Pearlie Mae and Jasper, the two black cats at Howard's Bookstore. The store's owners, Mary and Howard Canada, had every intention of taking the cat house back to their apartment. But the last I heard, they'd been overruled. The cat house was still in the bookstore window.

Pearlie Mae and Jasper are "just having the best time, and so are the customers. We're all enjoying this tremendously," Mary wrote. According to Mary, Pearlie Mae—who is a full six months older than Jasper—is taking full advantage of her seniority by claiming sole ownership of the top perch. When Jasper dares venture up, she slaps him. To save face, Jasper still insists on being first at the food dish.

Because the Skylight over Kitty Land has more heft than some of the previous units described, the plywood base should measure 20 inches by 20 inches. Carpet the top and sides of the base.

Working your way up from the bottom, start with the tunnel. You will need 24 inches of tubing to produce a 12-inch tunnel (see Tunnel of Love, pages 53–54).

The full unit will likely require three, and possibly four, tree limbs. For stability, level each limb across the bottom. As always, the more crooks and turns in your limbs, the more interesting the unit. In fact I once had a woman stop me at a cat show. "How did you get all those curves in that

Skylight over Kitty Land

tree?" she asked, looking at one of my cat houses.

With a mostly straight face, I replied, "Oh, I heated it up and shaped it."

"Real-l-l-l-y?" she said.

For stability, your principal tree-limb anchor limb should be 4 to 6 inches in diameter on the end that will be attached to the plywood base. Using six 20-penny sinker nails, hammer the limb several inches from one corner of the plywood base. Next attach the tunnel. Place it diagonally on the base, with the side of the tunnel against the limb. Using one 16-penny nail, hammer from the inside of the tunnel into the tree limb. More nails will be added later.

Moving up, the 20-inch full circle is on the next level. To construct a full circle, you will follow exactly the same procedure used to make a tunnel, but you won't cut away a 12½-inch section. You will leave the full circle as a full circle.

For your circle, take 40 inches of Sonotube. Saw the tube in half vertically to produce two 20-inch-long tubes. From one tube, remove a strip 1 inch wide and 20 inches long. Slip this smaller tube inside the other tube. Staple, tack, glue, or cement the tubes together.

For your jewel of a cat, the full circle gets a skylight. Cut a diamond shape in the tube, measuring 9 inches by 9 inches. If your cat enjoys crawling in and out of things, cut more than one diamond. Carpet the full circle inside and out.

When you attach the full circle to the tree limb, it will make no difference whether the diamonds are positioned at the top, on the sides, or in the bottom of the full circle. Just keep in mind that for ease of entrance and exit, the full circle should be about 18 inches from the floor. Also for maximum visual impact, you may want to select a particular crook or spot on the limb where the full circle seems to fit best. With one 16-penny nail, hammer from the inside of the full circle and into the tree limb. Depending on the curve of your tree limb, the circle will likely be hanging somewhere over the base.

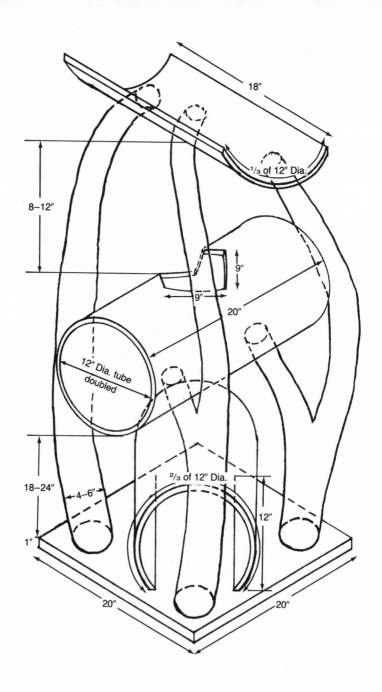

Skylight over Kitty Land

Saw off the top of the principal limb at whatever height is best for your room. To make the top perch, take 18 inches of paperboard tubing. Measuring the circumference along the inside of the tube, mark off three sections of 12½ inches apiece. Saw lengthwise so you end up with three 18-inch pieces. Staple, tack, glue, or cement two of the pieces together, one piece inside another. Save the third piece for your next perch. Carpet the perch. Nail the carpeted perch to the top of the tree.

Take a second tree limb approximately equal in length to the first. However, as this limb will be a brace limb and not a principal limb, its diameter does not necessarily have to be as great as that of the first limb.

Determine where this limb will need to be on the base so that it will touch the tunnel, the full circle, and the perch. Putting the unit on its side, use one 20-penny sinker nail to attach the center of this limb to the base.

Put the unit upright. Using 16-penny nails, attach the components to the second tree limb.

Turn the unit back on its side and anchor the second limb by hammering five 20-penny nails through the ply-wood base and into the limb. For stability and appearance, add at least one more limb. This will give you a tripod effect. The third limb should be in two parts. One section will reach from the top of the base to the bottom of the full circle. The other will extend from the top of the full circle to the bottom of the perch.

Now go back and recheck the entire unit. Add as many nails as necessary. Put on the soft music. It's time for Sky-light over Kitty Land.

CAT CONDO

CARPET DIMENSIONS REQUIRED: 12 feet by 5 feet
SONOTUBE: 3¹/₂ feet

Should your status-conscious feline crave a plush home on a wooded 20-by-20 lot, look no further. At do-it-yourself prices, a Cat Condo is a steal!

All construction techniques have been feline-tested. Start with two pieces of plywood measuring 20 inches by 20 inches. One piece will be the base. The other will be a platform on which your cat's private residence will sprawl. Carpet both pieces.

To spaciously accommodate all components, the principal limb of the cat house should be 3 or more feet long. For stability, cut the bottom of the limb straight across. Follow the same steps used in Tunnel of Love (see pages 53–56) to make a 12-inch-long tunnel and to attach the principal limb to the base and the carpeted tunnel to the limb.

A platform lot above the tunnel will provide the ideal setting for your cat's private residence. The prototype of this little house was a wooden box I once unceremoniously retrieved from someone else's trash. This was back when I first started selling scratching posts out of my carpet store in Fox River Grove. Inspired by the box, I mounted it on a tree limb, added carpet, and voilà! Here was my first big free-form cat house.

Exuberant, I displayed the result on the sidewalk in front of my store. About that time a fellow from the South Side of Chicago happened to walk by. He did a double take. Desperate for income, I took a deep breath. "Sir, that will be seventy-five dollars," I said, hardly believing my own ears. He wrote me a check.

Your costs, naturally, will be considerably less. But when it comes to luxury, your cat will never be short-changed. Among the condo's most glamorous features: a

A Cat Condo

graceful rooftop that serves as a skylight in winter and an air conditioner in summer. Year-round, it's a private entry/exit for agile felines.

For more mannerly and sedate cats—that is to say, those in need of a door—the front of the condo has an opening that measures 6 inches high and 8 inches long. Depending on how highly your cats regard themselves, you may wish to make this opening even bigger.

The Cat Condo has two durable plywood sides, measuring 12 inches long and 6 inches high. Two pieces form the sloping roof—one is 11 by 16 inches, and the other, which allows space for the skylight, measures 5 by 16 inches. No house for a slouch, this condo has a stately distance from platform to rooftop of 14 inches. For an even more detailed description, see the diagram on the facing page.

To assemble the condo, carpet all plywood pieces except the two sections that will make the condo roof; put those two sections aside. Tack together the roofless house. I recommend doing it this way because soon you will need to reach inside the house and attach the house to the platform lot.

Mount the platform on the principal tree limb at a height of about 12 to 18 inches from the ground. Here's a built-in safeguard against wear due to feline romps and stomps: At the spot on the limb where you wish to attach the platform, use your saw to cut a notch about 2 inches high and up to 2 inches deep. Slip the platform into the notch; anchor it with 16-penny sinker nails.

Now, as chief architect cum engineer, decide in which position the condo looks classiest on the platform. You may want a large front yard (if so, pull the front of the house near the back edge of the platform), a big backyard, a condo positioned diagonally, and so forth.

With 16-penny sinkers, nail the condo to the platform. Attach the two rooftop sections. Carpet these sections. In this way the rooftop carpeting can be wrapped down the sides of the condo for additional reinforcement. No wonder

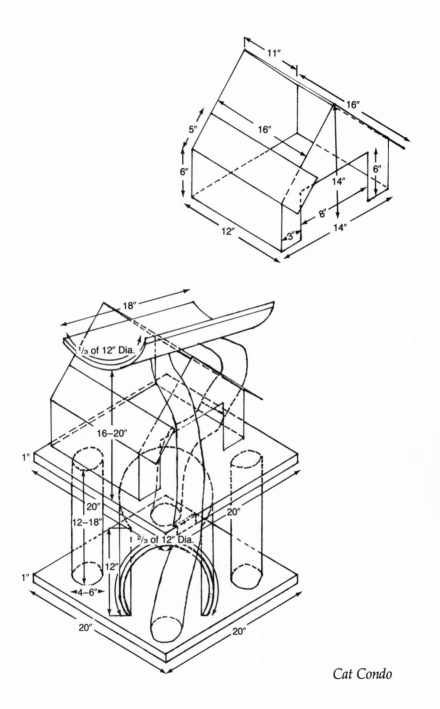

Cat Condo

this model gets the Good Catkeeping seal of approval.

With your saw, level the top of your principal tree limb. To make a perch, take 18 inches of Sonotube. Measuring from the inside and along the circumference, mark off three sections of approximately 12½ inches each. Saw the three sections lengthwise so you have three 18-inch pieces. Staple, tack, glue, or cement one piece inside another to make your perch. Carpet it. Save the third piece for another perch. With a 16-penny sinker, hammer the perch to the top of the tree limb.

Bracing the Cat Condo will require several short limbs. Two of these limbs should reach from the top of the base to the bottom of the platform. Another two should extend from the top of the platform to the bottom or sides of the perch. Measure the distances. Cut and attach the limbs.

Roll out the red carpet. Order catnip cookies and edible mice from Famous Fido Doggie Deli on the North Side of Chicago. It's time for open condo.

PERCH FOR FELINE SWINGERS

CARPET DIMENSIONS REQUIRED: 12 feet by 6 feet
SONOTUBE: 5½ feet

Remember the ecstasy of swinging on a backyard swing, feeling your body soar and fall to a rhythm just beyond control? Cats are swingers, too.

Consider Sioux, a white female. Sioux lives with four other cats and five cat houses. One of the cat houses has a swing; that's the house Sioux likes best. She's forever playing on it, swinging in it, and sleeping on it. Chances are, so will your cats.

The safest and most satisfactory feline swings, I've found, are boxes or builder's tubes open on just two sides or either end and dangling on a chain. How much dangle depends on how much chain you use and how far you wish the swing to swing.

Naturally, the addition of a swing to a cat house will add to the total weight of the unit and shift its center of gravity. Therefore, you will need to compensate:

1. The base of the cat house should be at least 20 by 20 inches.

2. To support the swing, select a principal tree limb of about 3 to 6 inches in diameter. So the swing can move freely without clunking into the rest of the cat's house or yours, this limb should be longer than the other limbs used to make the cat house. Moreover, the end of this particular limb should bend naturally at an angle of about 60 to 90 degrees. From this bend or curve, you will attach the swing.

3. Other limbs for the tree house should measure 4 to 6 inches in diameter.

Swinging perches can be added to a number of different cat houses. But two of my favorite Perches for Feline

Perch for Feline Swingers

Swingers are constructed by slightly modifying the Cat Condo and the Tunnel of Love.

The swing itself can be constructed of carpeted Sonotube or carpeted plywood. The plywood version requires four pieces of wood. The two pieces that will become the top and bottom of the swing should measure 12 inches by 15 inches. The two side pieces measure 10 inches by 15 inches. Nail the pieces together to form a box. Cats will be able to enter and exit through the open sides. If you have a small cat, you may wish to reduce the dimensions of the box.

A swing can also be made of Sonotube. Start with 24 inches of tubing. Cut it into two 12-inch sections. For extra strength, slice a strip 1 inch wide and 12 inches long from one of the tubes; slip this tube inside the other one. Staple, tack, glue, or cement the tubes together.

Put a screw eye (a screw with a head in the form of a loop) into the curved section of your longer or longest tree limb. Attach a chain with approximately 1-inch links to the screw eye's loop. Next, if you've made a wooden swing, drill a hole into the top of the wooden box and push in an eyebolt. Add a flat washer to the eyebolt, then a lock washer and a nut. The lock washer is an extra precaution. With continual use and enjoyment, the nut on the box will loosen and need to be tightened. The lock washer will help hold it in place longer. If your cat is a swinger, check the nut every day or so and retighten as necessary.

If your swing is made of builder's tubing, follow the accompanying diagram and cut away two flaps. This is where you will hang the swing. Add the eyebolt, lock washer, and nut, as above.

Now link the end of the chain to the ring of the eyebolt. If for some reason you don't wish to use a chain, substitute a large S-shaped hook to join the screw eye of the limb to the eyebolt of the box or tube.

Carpet the inside and outside of the box or tube.

Capture your cat's antics and reactions for posterity.

Keep a regular camera or a video camera handy. Satisfied cat house buyers from all over the country have filled the walls of my shop with snapshots of felines on their carpeted perches, tunnels, and houses. A number of those cats are swingers.

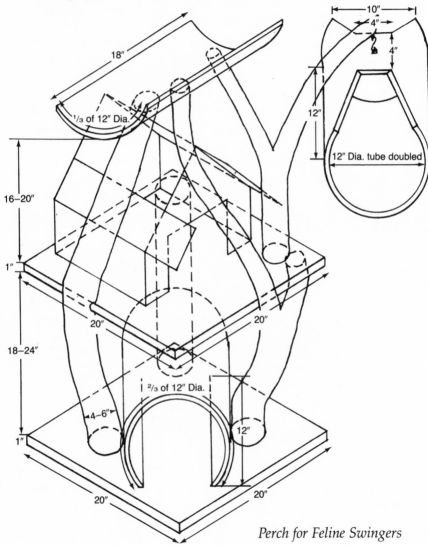

Perch for Feline Swingers

DOUBLE- AND TRIPLE-PERCH KITTY TREE HOUSES

CARPET DIMENSIONS REQUIRED: 12 feet by 5 feet to 12 feet by 6 feet
SONOTUBE: 5 feet

For topflight tabbies that go head over heels for heights, these models are heavenly. A tree house is an upscale kitty high rise. Space requirements at the ground level are minimal, but a tree house can accommodate floor after floor of kitty tenants.

Precisely how many "floors" depends on the length of your principal tree limb. This is the one that will reach from the base to the bottom of the top perch. For two perches atop a tunnel and house (see Cat Condo, pages 69–70), select a principal limb about 4 feet long. For three perches, your limb could span 5 or more feet.

A two-perch unit requires a section of carpeting 12 feet by 5 feet. For the three-perch unit, use a piece 12 feet by 6 feet.

For added support with both of these units, notch the principal limb where you plan to attach each perch except the top one; the top perch sits directly on top of the principal limb. Notch the limbs by sawing out an area up to 2 inches high and 2 inches deep. The platform will then slip into the notch, where it is securely anchored with 16-penny sinker nails.

Don't skimp on supporting limbs. These are the limbs that will go from the base to the bottom of the platform, and from the top of the platform to the top perch.

A well-occupied Double-Perch Kitty Tree House

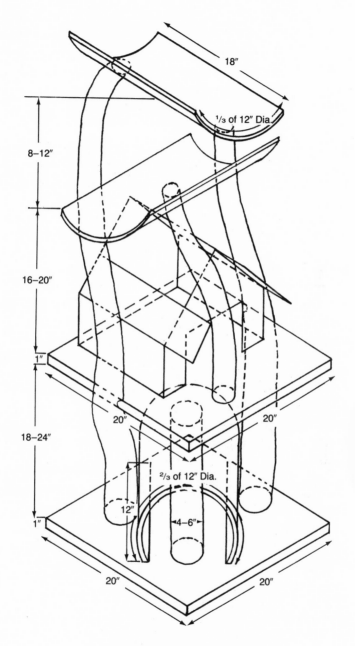

18"

⅓ of 12" Dia.

8–12"

16–20"

1"

20"   20"

18–24"

⅔ of 12" Dia.

12"

4–6"

1"

20"   20"

Double-Perch Kitty Tree House

KITTY DUPLEX

CARPET DIMENSIONS REQUIRED: 12 feet by 7 feet
SONOTUBE: 7 feet

The Kitty Duplex is ideal for an extended feline family. There is ample perch, play, and snooze space for Garfield, Felix, Fluffy, their pals, their broods, and all the homeless alley cats that wander by.

The Kitty Duplex utilizes several construction techniques used in earlier cat houses. This time you will need a plywood base and a plywood platform, each measuring 32 inches by 24 inches. Carpet the sides and tops of the base and platform.

For the first-floor base, build two carpeted tunnels. Each tunnel is 12 inches long (see Tunnel of Love, pages 53–54). Carpet the tunnels.

Because of the eventual heft of this unit, you will need two principal tree limbs. Each should have a diameter of 4 to 6 inches. Depending on your own floor plan, the limbs can be 3 to 5 feet tall. Level the bottom of the limbs and position them alongside the tunnels. Nail the base to the tree limbs with 20-penny sinker nails; use six for each limb. Nail the tunnels to the tree limbs with 16-penny sinkers.

About 18 to 24 inches from the first floor, attach the carpeted platform to your principal tree limbs. Using a handsaw and chisel, or light chain saw, make a notch about 2 inches high and 2 inches deep at the point on each limb where the platform will rest. Use 16-penny sinker nails to attach the platform to the limbs.

A distinctive Kitty Duplex house will be anchored to the second-floor platform. The side-by-side units of the plywood duplex will share a common wall. The units themselves are designed so that all the walls (fronts, backs, and sides) have the same dimensions. The walls are 14½ inches

The Kitty Duplex can accommodate many tenants.

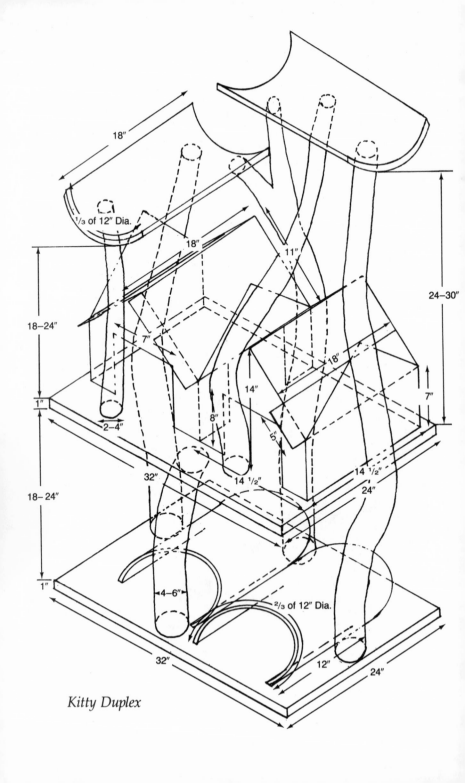

18″

¹⁄₃ of 12″ Dia.

18″

11″

24–30″

18–24″

7″

18″

14″

7″

1″

2–4″

8″

5″

18–24″

32″

14 ¹⁄₂″

14 ¹⁄₂″

24″

1″

4–6″

²⁄₃ of 12″ Dia.

32″

12″

24″

Kitty Duplex

long, and 14 inches from the bottom of the wall to the peak of the roof (see diagram on facing page).

Cut out seven identical plywood walls. On three of the walls, cut a doorway measuring 7 or 8 inches long and 8 inches high. Two of the doorways will be the front entrances to the duplex; the third is for the common wall between the units so that cats will have easy access to both sides. Carpet the plywood walls. Nail them together.

The duplex also has two skylight/air conditioners. Cut two pieces of plywood 11 inches by 18 inches; these will be the solid sides of the roof and will be anchored along the common wall of the two units. For an unusual effect, the units are designed so that the roofs sit inside the points of the walls. For the remainder of the roof, cut two pieces of plywood 18 inches by 5 inches; these sides will give a sky-light effect. Nail them in place and carpet the roof.

So there will be room for the cat company bound to drop by, construct and carpet two perches. Each will be 18 inches long. You will need 3 feet of Sonotube. Cut the tubing into two 18-inch sections. With each section, measure from the inside, along the circumference, and mark off three parts of approximately 12½ inches each. Saw the tubes length-wise. You will wind up with six pieces, each 18 inches long. For two perches, use four pieces. Save the rest for another cat house. For each perch, staple, tack, glue, or cement one piece inside another. Carpet the perch.

The perches should be nailed with 16-penny sinkers to the tops of your principal tree limbs. For a stepladder effect, you may wish to trim one of the trees down slightly so the perches are not anchored on exactly the same level. This will allow the cats to bound from one perch to another.

Brace the entire unit with as many tree limbs as you find necessary.

Brace yourself for a house—or a duplex—filled with felines.

Royal Cat-sle with defenders

ROYAL CAT-SLE

CARPET DIMENSIONS REQUIRED: 12 feet by 7 feet
SONOTUBE: 8 inches

United Press International once wrote: "A cat's home should be its cat-sle." For every feline lord, lady, baron, and baroness, this Royal Cat-sle is a humdinger.

Begin with two pieces of plywood. The base measures 32 inches by 35 inches. The platform on which the cat-sle will sit is 30 inches by 32 inches.

Before carpeting the plywood, consider feline protocol. Was this cat-sle a onetime Silver Tabby fortress purchased by an affluent Abyssinian and converted into a countryside retreat for her heralded progeny? If so, keep the carpeting nice and green. Or will this be a besieged cat-sle, likely to be attacked at any moment by intruder felines and intrusive humans? If so, you might opt for earth-tone coverings.

In addition, the Royal Cat-sle will soon have a drawbridge and a moat. For the moat, reserve a strip of blue carpeting for the platform.

Turn your attention to the platform. The cat-sle itself will have four identical sides, each measuring 20 inches long by 13 inches high. Naturally, cat-sle walls are crowned with battlements. How else would well-armed or well-heeled felines hurl catnip mice or kitty toys?

To make the crenels, or indentations, in the battlements, measure off 2 inches from both edges of each wall. For uniformity, all indentations will be 1 inch deep. There will be 2-inch merlons, or bumps, between each indentation. Since each wall measures 20 inches, measure two 2-inch merlons on each side, each with 2 inches in between. In the middle of the wall, this will leave a 4-inch merlon. You can cut crenels and merlons of any size you wish, but follow the same pattern on all four sides. If you prefer, make crenels and merlons on just the front and back sides.

For the cat-sle door, cut an opening 10 inches long and 10 inches wide. Carpet the walls. If you want the look of stone, use a gray or gray-flecked carpeting. Nail together the walls.

The cat-sle roof measures 20 inches by 20 inches and will sit inside the indentations of the walls. For those times when embattled felines need an additional path of escape, cut a hole 8 inches by 8 inches in the roof. Carpet the roof. Put it aside.

Tree-limb guard towers will anchor the cat-sle walls to the platform. Select four limbs about 4 inches in diameter and 16 inches high. Saw them off flat at both ends. If you

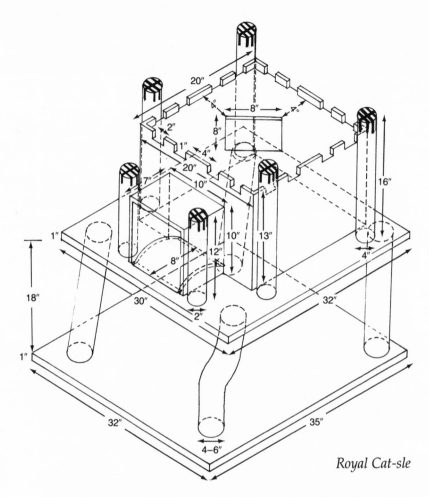

Royal Cat-sle

like, choose one limb somewhat larger than the others; this will be the donjon, or keep, which is a castle's most strongly fortified tower.

For heightened eye appeal, use your saw to make three parallel cuts across the top of the flattened tree-limb towers. Make one cut in the opposite direction. Use 20-penny sinker nails to hammer through the platform into each tower. Use 16-penny sinkers to attach the cat-sle walls to the towers. Attach the roof to the walls.

Pampered pets will need more fortification. An entry-way will shield the 10-by-10-inch door to the Royal Cat-sle.

For the entryway, cut three pieces of plywood 10 inches long and 7 inches high. Carpet them. Nail the entryway to the front of the cat-sle.

A feline version of a drawbridge uses a doubled Sonotube. As a space saver and a contoured walkway for cat-sle cats, the drawbridge may be slipped inside the entryway. Allowing for the thickness added to the entryway by the carpet on the plywood walls, cut two pieces of tubing 8 inches long and 8 inches wide; the latter measurement is the distance straight across, from one side of the tube to the other. Put one piece of tubing inside the other. Attach the tubes. Carpet the drawbridge.

Slip the drawbridge into the entryway. Staple, tack, glue, or cement it in place. Select two more tree-limb guard towers 2 inches in diameter and 12 inches high. Score them with the saw, as you scored the other limbs. With 16-penny sinker nails, reach inside the entryway and nail directly into the tree limbs. Don't forget to attach the blue moat.

Now, because we hold our cats in high esteem, we will elevate the Royal Cat-sle. Use four tree limbs 4 to 6 inches in diameter and 18 inches high. Level them off on both ends. Using 20-penny sinkers, anchor the limbs to the base and to the cat-sle-topped platform.

This Middle Ages structure should delight felines and humans of any age.

6

Luxury
Living for
Cats

$\mathbb{A}$s a do-it-yourselfer you have a prime opportunity to keep your cats living contentedly in the lap of luxury, and that lap need not necessarily be your own. For sweet-tempered felines there is probably no sweeter domicile than a gingerbread house. A fairy tale of a snoozing/scratching site, it's completely noncaloric.

GINGERBREAD HOUSE

CARPET DIMENSIONS REQUIRED: 12 feet by 7 feet
SONOTUBE: almost 7 feet

Although tree limbs on cat houses are normally never carpeted, on this house I make an exception. Just a few red and

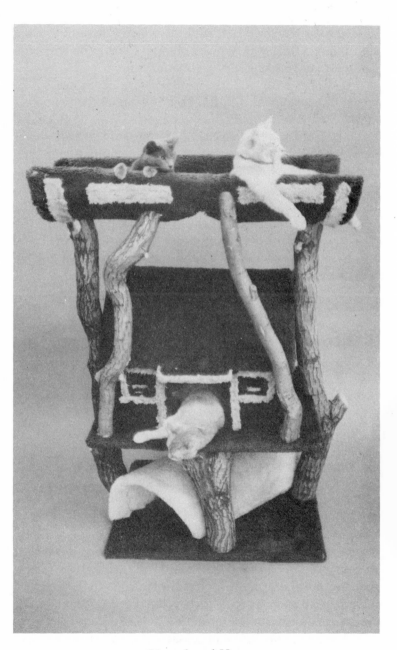

Gingerbread House

white strips wrapped here and there along the limbs give a candy-cane effect almost good enough to eat. The winsome Gingerbread House is a purrsonal favorite.

Both the base and the platform are 32 inches by 22 inches. Carpet them. On the base is a Sonotube tunnel 21 inches long (see Tunnel of Love, pages 53–54).

The front and back of the house measure 26 inches long by 11 inches high. In one of these pieces, cut an 8-by-8-inch doorway and a window on either side, measuring approximately 3 inches by 3 inches. The two sides of the house are 18½ inches long and measure 20 inches to the rooftop. The sides rise straight for 11 inches before sloping toward the roof (see diagram on facing page). Carpet the front, back, and sides. Use a different color, if you like, to highlight the windows and door.

For a whimsical rooftop effect, cut one piece of plywood 26 inches long and 16 inches high. Centered over your 8-inch-wide doorway will be a 9-inch flap. To do this, measure in 8½ inches from each side on your 26-inch-long piece of plywood roof; this will leave 9 inches in the center. Leaving the center portion intact, cut a 2-inch strip from the bottom on each of the 8½-inch sections. This means that on either side of the doorway, the rooftop measures 26 inches by 14 inches. Over the doorway, it remains 26 inches by 16 inches.

For the back of the roof, leave skylight/air conditioner space. Cut one piece of plywood 26 inches by 6 inches.

For a more compact effect, the base and platform have been cut the same size. The two principal tree limbs are 4 to 6 inches in diameter and 3½ to 4 feet high. Depending on the curve of the limbs, they will need to be anchored near the edge of the base and notched deeply enough to accommodate the platform. To notch the limbs, saw a section 2 inches high and up to 2 inches deep, exactly where the platform will rest on the limb.

Also, you may find it necessary to turn or trim a side of the tunnel so that the tunnel can be attached to the principal

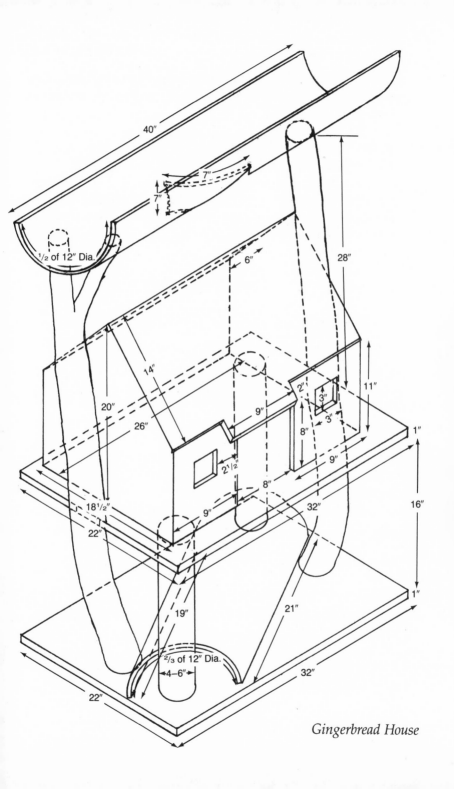

Gingerbread House

limbs. As always, use 20-penny sinker nails to attach the limbs to the base and 16-penny sinkers to nail the tunnel to both limbs.

Use 16-penny sinkers to attach the sides of the Gingerbread House to the principal limbs. Tack on the front and back of the house. Add the rooftop; carpet it.

For those cats with too much ginger to stay inside, construct a 40-inch perch that will rest between the two principal limbs (see Deluxe Scratch Pad, pages 46–49). Cut a diamond-shape entry/exit for your cat.

Sweet dreams.

World War I Biplane (Lafayette Es-Cat-Drille)

WORLD WAR I BIPLANE

CARPET DIMENSIONS REQUIRED: 8 feet by 3 feet
SONOTUBE: just over 5½ feet

I give Orville and Wilbur full credit for this one. I was scheduled to do a cat show in Dayton, Ohio. And how do you set foot in the hometown of the Wright brothers without an airplane for high-flying felines?

I can't promise that this World War I Biplane will remain aloft even twelve seconds, the duration of the Wright brothers' first airborne escapade. But I do know that it should provide your feline with many, many hours of enjoyment.

A floor-style cat house with no elevated perches, the biplane is ideal for older and less spry cats. It's also an eye-popping favorite in children's bedrooms.

The completed fuselage, or central body, of the plane is 34 inches long. Start with a 68-inch section of Sonotube. Cut

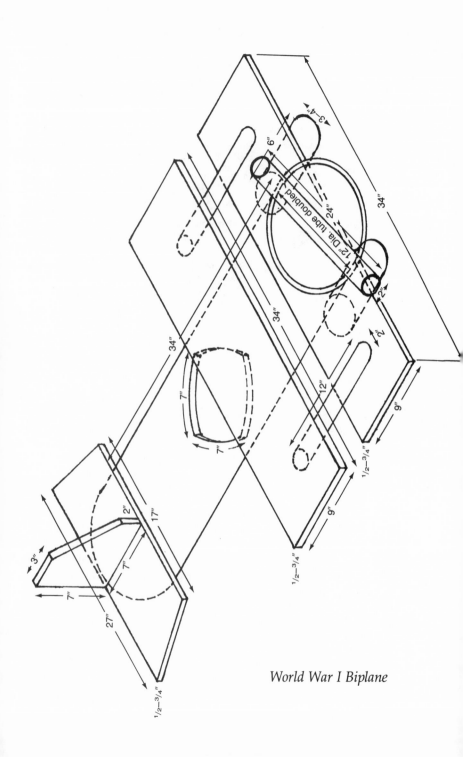

World War I Biplane

it into two 34-inch sections. In order to make the cat house last longer, one section of tubing will be placed inside the other. To do this, cut a strip from one tube 1 inch wide and 34 inches long; this tube will now slip inside the other tube. Staple, tack, glue, or cement the tubes together. Carpet the inside and outside of the fuselage.

For the kitty cockpit, locate the approximate center of the fuselage. Cut a diamond measuring 7 inches by 7 inches. Depending on where you wish to position the wings, this diamond shape could also be somewhat closer to the nose of the plane. Like all cockpits, this is an entry/exit for the pilot.

The plane has two wings. Use ½- to 1-inch-thick plywood. The wings are 9 inches by 34 inches. Carpet the wings. To attach the wings, reach inside the Sonotube fuselage and drive 16-penny sinker nails into the wings. To further stabilize your aircraft, add wing supports; use two tree limbs approximately 2 inches in diameter and 12 inches long. Nailed to the wings with 16-penny sinkers, these supports will clamp down tightly on the wings and hold them firmly to the body of the plane.

For the tail wing, measure a piece of plywood 27 inches on the back edge and 17 inches on the edge closest to the cockpit. The tail wing is 7 inches wide. For authenticity's sake, the tail needs a small fin. The fin is 7 inches high and 7 inches long. See the accompanying diagram for the slope of the fin. Carpet the tail and fin. Nail them in place.

For a feline pilot, a biplane needs a tree-limb propeller. The limb is 24 inches long and has a diameter of about 2 inches. To attach the propeller: Take a strip of carpeting, staple one end of the strip inside the Sonotube, and tightly wrap the carpet strip several times around the propeller. Staple, tack, cement, or glue the rest of the strip inside the tubing.

I wonder what Orville and Wilbur would think.

Hot Rod

HOT ROD

CARPET DIMENSIONS REQUIRED: 8 feet by 3 feet
SONOTUBE: 6¹/₂ feet

No pussyfooting around. This racy model is a tribute to fleet-footed felines. One woman who lived in a trailer was so smitten by the design that she special-ordered a souped-up version several feet longer than this one. How the car fit in her trailer, I've never been sure. But that wasn't my problem, or her speedster's.

Sleek-bodied, this hot rod starts with 68 inches of Sonotube. For extra strength, cut the tubing into two 34-inch sections. From one section, remove a strip 1 inch wide and 34 inches long. Slide this section into the other section. Staple, tack, cement, or glue the sections together. Carpet the body.

Sportive cats need a driver's seat. Into the tubing, cut a diamond shape 7 inches by 7 inches. For exhaust pipes, add two tree limbs measuring about 2 inches in diameter by 18 inches long. To attach them, reach inside the tubing and drive 16-penny sinker nails through the tubing and into the limbs. Should the nails penetrate all the way through the limbs, use your hammer to bend them around and back into the limbs. This will give additional support.

Two axles are likewise tree limbs—2 inches in diameter and 16 inches long. Again, reach inside the carpeted tubing and hammer into the axles with 16-penny sinkers. For eye-catching wheels, cut four 1-inch slices from a tree limb 6 inches in diameter. Hammer them in place with 16-penny sinkers.

If your cat gets his dander up, he'll need a windshield. Use more of the tubing. Cut off two sections that measure 10 inches from side to side and 5 inches deep. Staple, tack, cement, or glue one section inside the other, and carpet it.

To mount the windshield, use about a 2-inch wedge of tree limb. Nail it to the body tube just forward of the driver's seat and at the angle you wish your windshield to sit. Nail the windshield to the wedge.

Add carpet racing stripes. V-r-r-r-oom! V-r-r-r-oom!

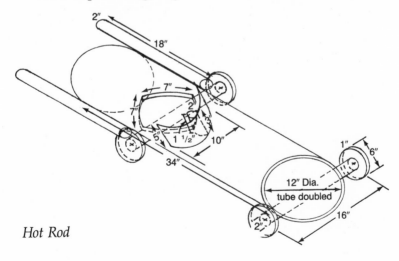

Hot Rod

SOUTHERN PLANTATION HOUSE FOR ARISTO-CATS

CARPET DIMENSIONS REQUIRED: 12 feet by 7 feet
SONOTUBE: 7 feet

For the laid-back life-style favored by many felines, a Southern Plantation House epitomizes gracious living. Aristo-cats shouldn't be needing any mint juleps on the veranda. But for lounging—or loping through a Virginia reel—felines will find ample space on a multitude of levels.

The top perches also allow easy accessibility by humans. The perches are ideal for times when, seeing our pets snoozing for the umpteenth hour of the day, we go over and rub their tummies. Invariably the cats give us an "Are you for real?" look, yawn, and go back to sleep.

In a Southern Plantation House, a cat will experience the finest in sleepin', playin', and livin'.

The plywood base for the unit measures 35 inches long by 22 inches wide. The plywood platform for the plantation house is 30 inches long and 22 inches wide. Carpet the tops and sides of both pieces.

You will need two principal tree limbs 4 to 6 inches in diameter and about 4 feet high. Level the base of the limbs.

For the tunnel on the base, cut a 48-inch section of Sonotube. Cut it in half (follow the directions for the Tunnel of Love, pages 53–54). Your finished tunnel of doubled tubing will be 24 inches long. Put the tunnel aside for now; later it will be attached to the supporting limbs.

The front and back sides of the plantation house are two rectangles 26 inches by 12 inches. In one of the pieces you've cut, center an 8-by-8-inch doorway, and cut two windows on each side of the door. This will allow Southern lady cats to watch for their gentleman callers. The windows should measure about 5 inches high and 2 inches wide.

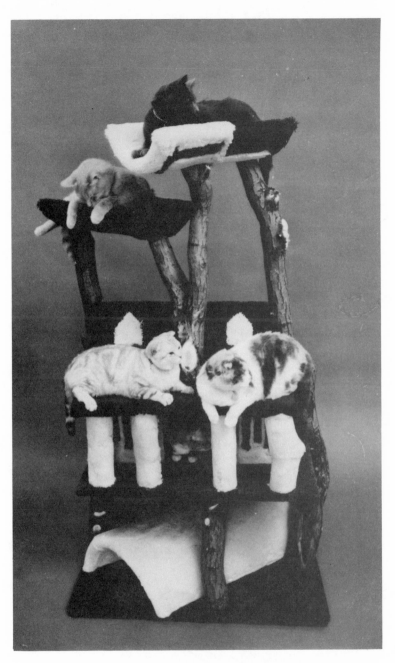

Southern Plantation House

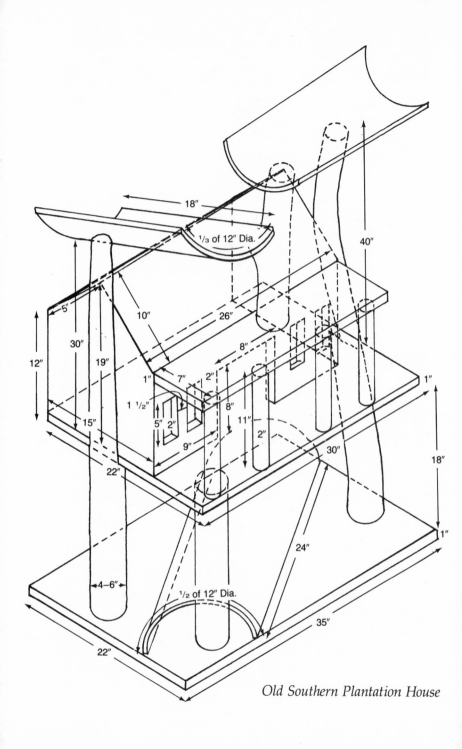

Old Southern Plantation House

The two sides of the plantation house are 15 inches long and measure 19 inches to the highest peak of the rooftop (see diagram on facing page). The sides are cut straight for 12 inches, then slope toward the rooftop point.

The plantation-house roof, like other cat house roofs, will have a skylight, which can double as an air conditioner. But depending on how many aging magnolias grow on the spacious lawn, aristo-cats may require no manufactured breezes. The side of the roof closest to the front of the plantation house measures 26 inches long by 10 inches high. The other side of the roof, which will have the skylight, is 26 inches long by 4 inches high.

For the veranda—and what's a plantation house without a veranda?—cut a roof 26 inches long by 7 inches wide.

Carpet all plywood plantation-house pieces except the roof and the veranda roof. For effective contrast, set off the windows and doorway, perhaps in brown carpet if the house is white, or vice versa.

Nail the front, back, and sides of the house together. Taking into account the 30-inch length of the platform that will hold the house, nail the principal limbs to the base with 20-penny sinker nails. To securely accommodate the platform, notch the principal limbs with a saw at about 18 inches from the floor; notches can be about 2 inches high and up to 2 inches deep. Slip the platform onto the limbs, anchoring the pieces together with 16-penny sinker nails.

Place the plantation house, minus the roof pieces, on the platform. With 16-penny sinkers, nail the house to the tree limbs. Then anchor the roof of the house to the principal tree limbs.

To anchor the veranda roof, select four pillar tree limbs 2 inches in diameter and 11 inches high. Level them off. Use 16-penny sinkers to nail the veranda roof to the pillars.

Carpet the plantation-house roof and the veranda roof. For additional support, you might pull some of the rooftop carpet down on the sides of the house. Also, add a couple of small white rectangular pieces of carpet to the front of the roof. These are your dormer windows.

Use tubing to construct and carpet two 18-inch-long perches. Because the tubes will be doubled, start with a total of 6 feet of tubing. Depending on the curve of your principal tree limbs, create a stepladder effect with the two perches. One will be attached to the top of each limb. Put the perches at different angles. You may want to shorten one of the limbs slightly.

Go back to the tunnel and the base. Take two support limbs 4 to 6 inches in diameter and 18 inches long. The support limbs will be anchored with 20-penny sinkers to the base and the platform. With 16-penny nails, attach the tunnel to the support limbs.

Now you're the one who's ready for a catnap.

CATNIP SALOON

CARPET DIMENSIONS REQUIRED: 12 feet by 7 feet
SONOTUBE: 3¹/₂ feet

Howdy, purrtner. Pussyfootin' cats better clear out of town. Don't go scratchin' your tummy against the bar 'less you're ready for a knock-down-claw-out fight. This, my feisty four-footed felines, is the Catnip Saloon.

The plywood base measures 32 inches by 24 inches. The platform is 30 inches by 24 inches. Carpet the tops and sides of the base and platform. The one principal tree limb for the saloon is 4 to 6 inches in diameter and about 4 feet high. Level it off at the bottom.

Using 24 inches of builder's tubing, construct a 12-inch tunnel (according to the directions in the Tunnel of Love, pages 53–54). Carpet the tunnel. With 20-penny sinker nails, attach the principal tree limb to one side of the base. Use 16-penny sinkers to nail the tunnel to the limb.

The two sides of the saloon measure 16 inches by 14 inches. The back is 21 inches by 16 inches. The front is 21 inches long and measures 24 inches to its peak; the sides of the front rise straight up for 21 inches before sloping in for the roof (see diagram on page 103). The front, which has a CATNIP SALOON sign, has to be high; how else are those no-account catpokes and cowcats gonna find their way? Carpet the sides.

In the front piece, cut an 8-by-7-inch doorway and two 4-by-4-inch windows. Like most saloons, this one has swinging doors. So sloshed cats don't get caught in the middle, the doors are permanently swung open. Cut two 4-inch squares of plywood. These are the doors. To keep them halfway open, insert a small plywood wedge behind them. Nail the doors and the wedge to the saloon.

The saloon's plywood rooftop is 28 inches by 21 inches. Measuring 16 inches from the back of the roof, cut out a

Hot time at the Catnip Saloon

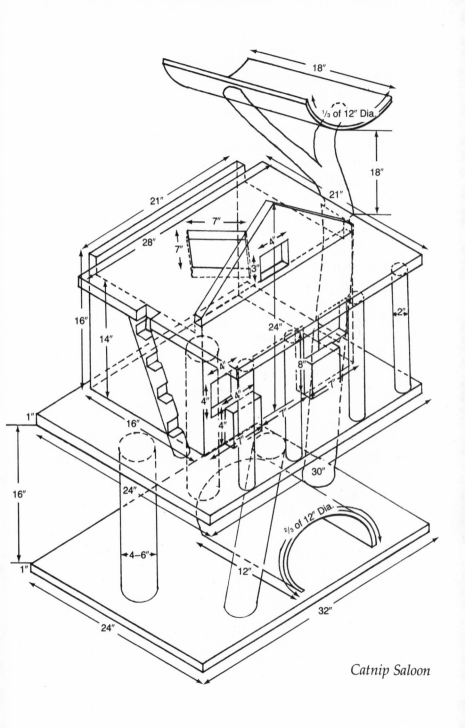

Catnip Saloon

2-inch horizontal section 21 inches long to slide over the peak of the roof; the space underneath will be the porch. In case the sheriff stages a raid, in the center of the roof cut a 7-by-7-inch diamond-shape escape hatch.

Notch the principal tree limb about 16 inches from the ground. Saw a spot 2 inches high and up to 2 inches deep. Slide the platform into the notch. Anchor one side of the saloon to the principal tree, using 16-penny sinker nails. Tack together the other sides of the saloon. Pull the rooftop down over the peak on the front of the saloon, and using 16-penny sinkers, anchor the rooftop to four supporting tree-limb hitching posts. The posts measure about 2 inches in diameter and 13 inches high. Carpet the roof, which extends about 5 inches over the front of the saloon.

For desperado cats, better add a side stairway. Take a short limb about 2 inches in diameter. With a saw, notch one side of it to look like steps. Tack the limb at an angle to one side of the saloon. Where the stair limb meets the rooftop, cut a 1-inch notch/stair in the roof.

For gambling and gamboling cats, top the saloon with a private 18-inch-long Sonotube perch/off-limits club room. Attach the carpeted perch to the principal tree limb.

Add supporting limbs 4 to 6 inches in diameter between the base and the platform. Hammer them with 20-penny sinker nails.

Let's hope your felines take care of this place. It's too purrty for shoot-outs.

Casey Cat and his fireman

KITTY CHOO-CHOO

CARPET DIMENSIONS REQUIRED: 8 feet by 3 feet
SONOTUBE: nearly 7 feet

This is a dual-purpose cat house—ideal for felines that chug through life or those known to get steamed. Moreover, the overall design makes the Kitty Choo-Choo a favorite in children's bedrooms.

For the front of the engine, start with a 40-inch section of Sonotube. Cut it in half to produce two 20-inch pieces. From one of these pieces, cut a strip 1 inch wide and 20 inches long. Slide this smaller tube inside the larger one. Fasten the tubes together as described previously. Carpet the tube.

For the cab where your kitty engineer will perch, you will be making a tunnel, then tacking it upright. Start with 42 inches of Sonotube. Follow the same procedure used above and construct a 21-inch tube. Then on the inside of this tube, take a tape measure along the rim (this would be the circumference of the tube) and mark off a 12½-inch

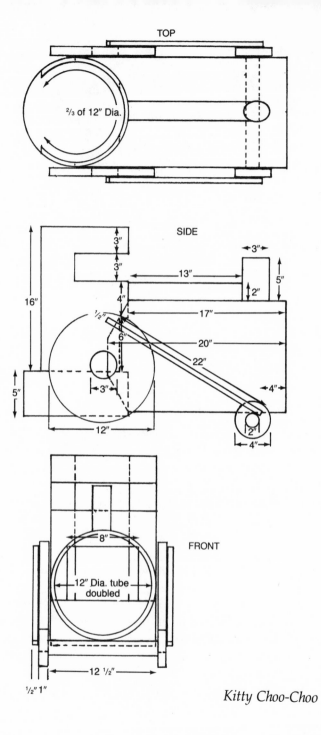

Kitty Choo-Choo

section. Saw away this section, which is 12½ inches wide and 21 inches long; save this as a customized perch for another cat house. Carpet the doubled tube.

The 21-inch tunnel will sit inside the 20-inch tube, one tube perpendicular to the other. Keeping in mind the dimensions of the tunnel tube, cut a circle to accommodate it toward the back of the 20-inch tube. For stability, cut this circle through what will be both the top and the bottom of the tube. Squeeze the cab (the tunnel-shaped Sonotube) all the way through the engine tube. The cab will be in an upright position. This will be anchored by the large back wheels, or driving wheels.

To make the driving wheels, cut two 12-inch plywood circles. Nail the driving wheels through both the engine and the cab.

Your kitty will need good visibility. Assist the engineer by cutting a circular piece of plywood to sit horizontally inside the cab. Carpet this seat.

For the front wheels, or pilot wheels, cut two 1-inch-thick circles from a tree limb with a diameter of 4 inches. For the front axle, cut a 15½-inch section of tree limb about 2 inches in diameter. With 16-penny sinkers, nail the front wheels to the axle.

Trains need smokestacks. Cut a 5-inch chunk from a tree limb 3 inches in diameter. This is your smokestack. Reach inside the Sonotube and nail it with 16-penny sinkers to the engine. For speedy access to equipment by the crew, the locomotive needs a narrow running board. Cut a 13-inch strip from a tree limb measuring about 2 inches in diameter. From the inside, nail the running board to the engine. Toenail, or angle, a 16-penny sinker from the running board into the smokestack.

Using two pieces of plywood measuring ½ inch wide by ½ inch thick, measure two 22-inch-long connecting rods. On either side of the engine, they will connect the driving wheel to the pilot wheel.

Choo-choo! Chug-chug!

DOOR SAVER

CARPET DIMENSIONS REQUIRED: 1 foot by 2 feet

This is not a house. But depending on your cat's manners, it could well help save yours. Every time some house cats wish to scat off and roam outdoors, they scratch impatiently against the door. Unlike even grimy fingerprints, which stand some chance of being wiped clean, these scratches defy removal. And weeks, months, or years of scratching on the same spot renders the scrapes deeper and deeper. Hence the Door Saver.

Take a piece of plywood 6 to 8 inches wide and 24 inches long. Carpet it. With carpeting or clothesline, make a loop large enough to fit over the doorknob. Staple, glue, or cement the loop to the top of the plywood.

Consider this a scratch pad/memo pad. Your feline will continue to signal "I want to get outside," but your door won't be sacrificed in the process.

The Door Saver can of course also be hung against any wall that for one reason or another is subjected to frequent scratching.

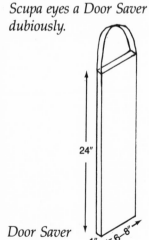

Scupa eyes a Door Saver dubiously.

24"

Door Saver

1" 6–8"

7

Dreams-for-Sale Cat Houses

Human beings sacrifice and scrimp for years for a dream house. And then just when they're ready to call the real estate agent, interest rates jump. With felines, you'll have no such cat-astrophes.

Unleash your imagination. A carpeted wooden box mounted in a tree limb becomes a Secluded Siamese Summer House. A large box and a small box carpeted and nailed together double as a suburban ranch house with an attached garage, or a cat château with measly mouse quarters.

Budget, for once, is no limitation. Whether you splurge or cut corners, you can still construct something splendid.

Either conjure up your own ideas, purrsonalize one of these, or further customize a cat house you've already built or bought.

And don't forget:

1. Somewhere in your design, incorporate one or more tree limbs.

2. If you're building a larger unit, aim for a stepladder effect with perches and various components on different levels. Cut skylight/air conditioners and diamond-shape openings wherever cats may need additional entries and exits.

3. Carpet all cat house surfaces except tree limbs and the bottom of the base. Also, if the bottom of any platforms used are not visible to you when they're positioned on the principal tree limbs, don't carpet them.

4. Tighten or add nails and supporting limbs as necessary. To securely anchor a platform, notch the tree limb that will support it.

5. Beware of making the cat house so small or the perches so close that you'll cramp your cat's style.

6. Beware of making the cat house so big you'll need to build on to your home in order to accommodate it. (I ran into a similar problem the last time I built a Royal Cat-sle. Elated over the turrets and the drawbridge, I totally forgot about modern-day limitations. On the way to putting the castle in my van, I was thwarted by an immovable foe—my doorway. The castle was too big to carry out of my shop.)

The following ideas are among those I've collected over the years from customers, friends along the cat-show circuit, and business associates. What these people share is an abundant love of cats, whimsy, and the ability to maximize their pets' enjoyment—and their own.

One customer in particular could have been the mega-builder of the cat world. His preference, at least for feline residents, was a four-unit apartment with a penthouse. Thanks to my scavenging, I was able to deliver quickly.

Earlier, from alongside the road on one of my drives to and from the shop, I had salvaged a discarded chest of drawers. I figured I'd need it someday.

All aboard!

Converting my find to a cat-size apartment required removing all the drawers. To divvy up future living space, I nailed in one horizontal plywood partition. The partition was centered and spanned from one side of the empty chest to the other. Now there were two "apartments." To make four, I sawed a tree limb in half so that part of it reached from the top of the horizontal plywood partition to the top of the chest. The other part reached from the bottom of the horizontal partition to the bottom of the chest. The limbs were centered and nailed in place. No longer would pampered cat tenants have to venture outside to scrape their paws.

The next installation was wall-to-wall floor-to-ceiling interior and exterior carpeting. Had the frame of the chest of drawers not been assembled when I started, I would have carpeted the pieces first, then nailed them together; usually this makes for a neater assembly process.

One touch remained. The gentleman wanted his top dog/cat to have a penthouse. My version was a small sloping-roofed cat house (see Cat Condo, pages 68–70). I nailed it to the top of the chest. All in all, the finished product was top-drawer.

From Charlene Whitney comes the idea of suspending toys from a cat house. Charlene understands kitty psyches as well as anyone I've ever met. She is a tireless worker for Helping Paws, an organization in Crystal Lake, Illinois, that finds homes for abandoned animals.

Although allergic to cats, Charlene has taken in eighty of them over the last three years. Many were barely alive. Charlene hand-raises them until they're well enough to be adopted. She feeds them every two hours around the clock. And when they're strong enough to play, she puts them in her cat houses.

To extend the cat houses' innate appeal, Charlene adds dangling cat toys. Felines love to bat objects with their paws. An easy way to attach a cat toy to a house is with a screw eye, which comes with its own loop. Put the screw eye directly into the tree limb of your cat house. Hang the cat toy from the screw eye with a piece of nylon rope or twine. Many toys already have their own loops and can therefore easily be attached. Otherwise simply wrap and tightly tie the rope or twine several times around the toy. Many cat toys are cushiony and will hold easily in place. Naturally, make sure that the rope is short enough to prevent the cat from becoming entangled, and that the toys have no parts that could be swallowed.

Charlene also advises that toys not be hung with yarn, foil-wrapped string, or any material that a cat might be tempted to bite through or ingest.

To see Charlene's own cat, Cupcake, jubilantly swat six or eight toys—each dangling from its own screw eye—you'd never know she was once a screaming, homeless, shivering kitten. To make sure she doesn't shiver any more, Charlene tucks a soft blanket into Cupcake's cat house on chilly nights.

One of the most unusual cat houses I've ever seen was brought to me by a onetime employee. He would tell me only that he had a surprise; he was right. Using builder's tubes, he constructed a three-foot-tall Trojan horse. The horse had a full tube for the body, smaller tubes for the legs, assorted entry and exit hatches, and a carpet saddle and bridle. Though cats could hide inside, there was nothing timid about the asking price of $150. We sold the unit.

Dream on. That's how I came up with the following:
BOOKWORM CAT. This is the feline equivalent of self-publishing. Start with a base and a tree-limb scratching post. For the perch, take two plywood rectangles. These are the front and back covers of the book. Carpet them. For the book's spine, cut a long narrow piece of carpeting and attach it to one edge of the book's covers. Books have authors. Cut out your cat's name in a contrasting color of carpeting and staple or glue it to the spine. The unit makes a nice cat perch for your library.

PYRAMID CAT. It has been said that a razor blade inside a

Tasha in her library

pyramid retains its sharpness. When I was struggling to teach Tasha her first tricks, I used to tease that I would put her in a pyramid to sharpen her up. With speed that would have stunned the ancients, you can construct your own pyramid by sawing a rectangular plywood base and four triangular plywood sides. Carpet all surfaces.

Egyptian pyramids were carefully sealed. Yours will need to have several openings for your cat. A cat in a pyramid is quite appropriate. Egyptians worshiped cats, protected them by law, and memorialized them in art.

Bastet, a female cat goddess, was credited with controlling fertility in humans and livestock. To kill a cat was punishable by death. And when cats died, Egyptians had them mummified, along with the remains of mice and rats for mummified munchies in the hereafter. In contrast, your chief concern is your cat's current needs. Somewhere on or within the pyramid, attach a tree-limb scratching post.

CIVIL WAR CAT. You won't find this on many battlefields. But it could prevent your chair and table legs from being turned into a feline war zone. For the tubular portion of the cannon, start with 28 inches of tubing: cut the tube in half. Slice off a 1-inch lengthwise strip from one section and fasten it inside the other tube. The finished cannon will be 14 inches long. Mount the tube to a tree-limb carriage. Add four carpeted plywood wheels.

CLOWN CAT. Cats get to scratch and snooze. You get the laughs. If the clown is constructed carefully, there will be no pratfalls. The clown's face is a Sonotube. Carpet it. Add carpet eyes and carpet rouged cheeks. Cut out plywood ears and a large nose. Anchor it all to a principal tree limb attached to a base.

WIGWAM CAT. Copy the Indians: Use tree limbs for your central structure. Mount the limbs on a carpeted plywood base. Skip the animal hides on the exterior. Instead, use carpet. But first attach small pieces of plywood to the tree limbs. Staple or tack the carpet to the plywood. Cut a front flap. No need for smoke signals. You'll know when Chief Cat is home.

WISHING-WELL CAT. For good luck in his dream house, your feline might take a trip to the wishing well. Start with 24 inches of Sonotube. Cut the tube in half and slip one section into the other as described in Civil War Cat above. Carpet the tubing. To a carpeted plywood base, nail two tree limbs about 3 feet high and 4 to 6 inches in diameter. One of these tree limbs will be on either side of the tube. You'll want to hang a "bucket" at the top. To do so, drill a hole about 1½ inches in diameter, into each principal tree limb. The holes should be 18 inches from the floor, and on the side of the limbs facing the middle of the tube. Into the holes, insert a tree limb about 1½ inches in diameter and 12 inches long. Wrap this limb with rope. Leave a small portion of the rope hanging down. Rather than hanging a bucket, attach a toy.

Nail a carpeted platform to the tree limbs. Make a wish.

Happy landings!

Epilogue: Unexpected Rewards

Cats have always had me wrapped around their little paws. I'd do anything for them. But as a cat house builder, I've somehow managed to touch their lives—and the lives of their humans—in ways I never expected.

There's a dog named Candy, a tail-wagging, tongue-licking sort, who lives with a bunch of kittens. Candy is the kittens' best protector and playmate. Invariably when the kittens are on their Tunnel of Love cat house, so is Candy. As the kittens playfully whomp each other off their carpeted tunnel, she's there to retrieve them. Humans in the household, touched by this canine-feline togetherness, snapped photos. Each one shows Candy and her kittens sharing the Tunnel of Love cat house.

Janet Fink has found human imagery in cat furniture.

Animals are like people, she says. "They need a place where no one will touch them and no one will bother them."

Janet's household includes eight cats and two cat houses. "When the cats are in their cat trees," she says, "I don't allow them to be petted. My children are grown now. But even when young children are in the house, I make sure they know the cat trees are the cats' special place."

Not long ago, there was a mother-to-be cat. A fresh box had been placed in a bedroom for her. In the same bedroom was her Cat Condo. Respecting her privacy but eager to assist in any way, family members would periodically hover. But as things turned out, the cat needed no labor coach or midwife.

As her time neared, the cat sequestered herself in the little carpeted, sloping-roofed house of her Cat Condo. Instinctively she converted it into a birthing room. That's where she delivered her kittens.

If ever a cat house was an honest-to-goodness refuge and home, that was it.